THEIR RIGHTS AND LIBERTIES.

the beginnings of religious and political freedom in Maryland

BY THOMAS O'BRIEN HANLEY, S.J.

DEPARTMENT OF HISTORY, MARQUETTE UNIVERSITY

A Campion Book

LOYOLA UNIVERSITY PRESS • CHICAGO, ILLINOIS

6-16-88 dmi

Copyright ©1984 LOYOLA UNIVERSITY PRESS

Library of Congress Cataloging in Publication Data

Hanley, Thomas O'Brien.
  Their rights and liberties.

  Reprint. Originally published: Westminster, Md.:
Newman Press, 1959. (With a new subtitle).
  Bibliography: p. 131
  Includes index.
  1. Religious liberty—Maryland—History. 2. Church and state—Maryland—History.
3. Maryland—Church—history. I. Title.
BR555.M3H3 1984   322'.1'09752   84-11265
ISBN 0-8294-0471-6

        Imprimi potest: LEO J. BURNS, S.J.
                Provincial Superior
                May 15, 1958

Nihil obstat: JOHN A. SCHULIEN, S.T.D.   *Imprimatur:* WILLIAM E. COUSINS, D.D.
  Censor Librorum   Archbishop of Milwaukee
  July 19, 1959   August 22, 1959

        Originally published in 1959 by THE NEWMAN PRESS
        Library of Congress Catalog Card Number: 59-14758
        Printed in the United States of America

TO
MY PARENTS

"The Inhabitants of this Province shall have all their rights and liberties according to the Great Charter. . . ." —THE MARYLAND ORDINANCE OF 1639

FOREWORD

THE PROBLEM of defining the rights of the church and of the state and of determining the obligations of citizens to each of these institutions has been one of the most difficult and controversial in the history of Western civilization.

Totalitarian governments have attempted to do away with the problem by affirming that the only allegiance of the citizen is to the state. They have, of course, not succeeded entirely, as the current struggle in the communist dominated countries bears witness. But in the democracies, the problem has not yet been fully solved. It seems that we must anticipate the continued existence of a kind of "no-man's land" in which the line of separation will not be clear. Here the line must be determined on the basis of personal freedom in the spirit of the Ninth Amendment.

The allegiance of the citizen is not a divided one, but rather a dual one: on the one hand to his Creator and to the divine law— which ultimately transcends any human decree; on the other hand, as a member of human society, to civil authority. The obligations to church and state meet in the conscience of every person. New circumstances produce new situations in which the precedents and practices of the past can help, but cannot fully remove the necessity for prudential judgment and adjustment.

Thomas O'Brien Hanley, S.J., in his book entitled *Their Rights and Liberties,* has undertaken to reconstruct the steps by which the Maryland colonists from 1634 to 1649 reversed the prevailing European doctrines and policies regarding the state and its relationship to religion and individual conscience. The colonists in

v

Maryland substituted for royal absolutism a representative government based on the consent of the people. They replaced an established church, accompanied by suppression of religious dissidents,
with a society which allowed for religious differences and toleration.

Such sharp breaks with tradition, of course, do not emerge suddenly. One of the special merits of Father Hanley's work is his
sketch of the history of English thought and controversy which
helped to clarify the church-state relationship and which provided
a basis in principle for the Maryland experiment.

The tragic religious wars and persecutions of the sixteenth and
seventeenth centuries arose in large part from a genuine confusion on all sides as to the principles which should regulate relationships between church and state. The things of Caesar and
the things of God were badly mixed. Conscientious men were
seeking answers to questions such as these: Did the church have
power to release its members from their obligations to the state?
Did the state have the right to require citizens to take an oath of
allegiance to the state and also to the religion which the ruler
professed? Was religious heresy a civil crime or was religious
dissidence the equivalent of treason? With the good and wise
men unable to agree upon the answers to these questions, the way
was left open for unwise and sometimes malicious men to abuse
both church and state.

Yet, out of the tragedy, a new concept emerged. In part it was
a return to the principle of the "Two Powers" which had been
affirmed as early as the fifth century by Pope Gelasius. It reflected,
too, the common medieval principle that the ruler's power had to
be approved by "consent of the people." It also involved a new
application of the English common law tradition of the rights and
liberties of individual citizens, expanded to include the right to
freedom of conscience in religious faith.

Father Hanley's book is valuable as a record of the development of these principles, and perhaps even more valuable because

while developing this record, it gives clear lessons in the technique of effective political action. It illustrates that politics is the art of the possible and that in difficult times the exercise of great restraint and great prudence is essential. This is clearly indicated in the record of the years of efforts of Lord Baltimore and his son to establish a colony in Maryland. A convert after he had attained his office, George Calvert stayed in favor with Charles I because he was a loyal royalist. Lord Baltimore saw the possibilities of providing a haven for his Catholic countrymen in a colony removed from the tensions of the homeland. Working within the existing structure of government, he prepared the way for the granting of a favorable charter to his son which was received after the death of the first Lord Baltimore. Neither father nor son aimed at complete perfection or at the ideal, which was impossible in England at that time, but they aimed at what could be obtained.

The securing of civil rights is a hard, slow process. This is clearly shown in the history of the Maryland colonists. Isolated in the New World, they had freedom to experiment and to assert claims which were unthinkable in England at that time and which brought objections from the patrons as well as from the crown. The Maryland Ordinance of 1639 is remarkable both for its assumption of the principle of "consent of the people" and for the way in which the assemblymen trimmed away phrases and sections of Lord Baltimore's code so as to, in effect, provide for religious toleration.

The history of the Maryland colony indicates too that good things once obtained must be carefully guarded and nurtured. The Maryland experiment in toleration was threatened when Puritans, both in England and in the colonies, became overly zealous to make the laws more "orthodox."

In the United States, of course, we have a constitutional guarantee of religious toleration in the First Amendment which is strengthened and supported by 170 years of tradition. There is no serious threat to religious freedom in the United States today. There are other areas, however, in which there is a disposition to deny to the accused and to the unorthodox their procedural rights and to extend the authority of the state into the realm of ideas and possible attitudes, rather than limiting it to overt acts.

Father Hanley's book is the clear story of the manner in which wise men undertook successfully to obtain and secure basic human rights.

EUGENE J. McCARTHY

The United States Senate
WASHINGTON, D. C.
March 12, 1959

PREFACE

*New Edition for the Three Hundred and Fiftieth Anniversary of the
Founding of Maryland* (1634-1984)

"THE CATHOLIC TRADITION OF FREEDOM IN MARYLAND"

Twenty-five years ago, American historians were developing a methodology in social and intellectual history. The Catholic community at the same time was making an historical
evaluation of its church-state teaching and what new light the
American experience gave to this. John Courtney Murray, S.J.,
played a major role in this effort which emerged in the Vatican
Council II declaration of religious freedom. His writings and
those of Merle Curti on intellectual history influenced my
approach to the record of early Maryland.

The story developed here hinges on the understanding that
there are historical traditions of freedom which are articulated
from one generation to another. They stand as a significant force
beyond the explicit provisions in law. The central episode here
is in the Maryland Assembly in 1639 and the ordinance it formulated. As an articulation by a Catholic leadership it throws light
on a church-state tradition, even though it did not decisively determine the final formulation of law on religious freedom. At the
same time it will be seen how that tradition had an influence on
the interpretation of the English legal formulae that *were* put on
the books. This thrust might best be stated as a belief that
religious freedom is a civil right: the toleration act in the ordi-

nance of 1639 contained no such reservation as the phrase
"being Christian," which Lord Baltimore's code contained and
which is again found in the Toleration Act of 1649 that became
law.

This law therefore does not accurately reflect the tradition
articulated by the Catholic assemblymen in 1639 and others
thereafter. At least this is true where the "being Christian" reservation is concerned. Where the Toleration Act of 1649 says, however, that no one shall be disturbed in the free exercise of
religion, it expresses the understanding of Catholics in England
at the time the settlers left for Maryland. It is this statement, without any reservations, which is often referred to in later articulations of the Catholic community in Maryland through the
eighteenth century. On this basis the title of the story given here
can be considered to have another sub-title in addition to what
it has: "The Catholic Tradition of Freedom in Maryland." This was
presented in summary and explicit terms shortly after publication of the book. Other writers have since followed it. In some
cases new instances and articulations of it have been noted. On-
going research should in addition uncover the context of the
articulations as well as the logical relationships among them.
This is what has been done here with the 1639 ordinance in full
detail.

In 1961 Justice Hugo L. Black, in writing the majority opinion in *Torcaso v Watkins,* cited the story given here and placed
it in a broader context. "There were wise and far-seeing men,"
he said of the first Maryland assemblymen and others at that
time, "who spoke out against test oaths and all the philosophy
of intolerance behind them." The historical reference was used
in his reasoning against the Maryland Constitution's requirement that public office holders profess belief in God. He noted
the state constitutional provision of 1776 which originally required profession of belief in Christianity, as well as the relief
given Jews in an 1825 amendment calling only for profession
of belief in God.

Mr. Justice Black still found a violation of religious freedom in the amended constitution, which was not in the full spirit of the Maryland founders. "The power and authority of the State of Maryland," he reasoned, "is put on the side of one particular sort of believers—those who are willing to say they believe in the 'existence of God'." This violated the First Amendment of the Federal Constitution. The Maryland law was struck down.

At the time of the court decision, Thomas H. Clancy, S.J., developed advanced research at the University of London on church-state thought in the English Catholic community from which Maryland assemblymen came. His careful study of Robert Persons (Parsons) established that the Jesuit controversialist in his last publication advocated the kind of church-state separation found in the ordinance of 1639. In particular, full civil and religious freedom for Jews and heretics was advocated. This gives important support and detail for the English background I have presented here. Thus, taken with recent advanced study of the Calvert family, additional enlightenment is gained on the English background as it impinged on the Maryland scene and the Catholic tradition of freedom.

Currently John D. Krugler is directly concerned with this connection. He makes it clear for the first time that the Calverts principally intended to apply current English legal formulae to Maryland—and not the church-state theory that emerged in the Catholic community with Persons and other writers. This does much to explain Cecil Calvert's code as discussed below and why the assemblymen's toleration act of 1639 was put aside. (See page 108.) It also explains why he accepted the 1649 Toleration Act with its reservation, "being Christian." All of this did not mean, however, that the Calverts rejected in theory the church-state separation statements made in the Catholic community in England and America.

Recently there has been quantitative research on the first settlers of Maryland. The ideological identity of the 1639 assemblymen with English Catholic church-state thought is clear. The

number of Catholics, on the other hand, as the principal influence in the assembly has now been clarified. By implication
Susan Rosenfeld Falb indicates there was a dominance by Catholics. Not that they were a numerical majority, but they held the
leadership and committee influence from which came the ordinance of 1639. Since all freemen were able to sit as
assemblymen, Protestants were numerically superior, but the
proxy system had Catholics holding the votes of Protestants
who designated them. These considerations confirm the interpretation followed below and the evidence of ideological
identity.

In tracing the Catholic tradition of freedom in Maryland
into the eighteenth century, account has been taken of the
Carroll families, for three generations leaders of their community. I turned from the present study to a construction of religion
during the revolutionary era in Maryland; and from 1963 to 1968
to a cultural biography of Charles Carroll, for his remarkable col-
lection of personal papers illuminates these times. In editing
the personal papers of John Carroll and after that in writing a second Charles Carroll volume, I found considerably more detail
for the tradition of freedom told here. The Maryland State
Constitution's article to protect all citizens from being disturbed
in the free exercise of their religion came from a committee on
which Charles Carroll sat. Its draft, however, contained the requirement that public office holders profess belief in the Christian religion. To Carroll, this smacked too much of a test oath.
In my earlier volume I noted the exchange he had with Sir
William Graves, M.P., where he expressed hostility to all oaths
touching religious belief. John Carroll opposed legislation that
would pay the salary of clergymen, and his articulations elsewhere on church and state are stronger for separation than in
Persons.

Thomas O'Brien Hanley, S.J.

References: Author, on "Catholic Tradition of Freedom in Maryland" in the *Catholic Mind* (Mar., 1963); "Church and State in Maryland . . ." *Church History* (Dec., 1957); *Charles Carroll* . . . (2. vols.; Loyola U. Press, 1983-84); *The John Carroll Papers* (3 vols.; U. of Notre Dame Press, 1976); *The American Revolution and Religion: Maryland 1770-1800* (Catholic U. of America Press, 1971). John D. Krugler, the *Maryland Historical Magazine* (Spring, 1984), which also has references useful in the above. Susan Rosenfeld Falb, Ph.D. diss., (Georgetown U., Dept. of History, 1976). Thomas H. Clancy, S.J. *Papal Pamphleteers* (1964).

ACKNOWLEDGMENTS

THE AUTHOR would like to express his gratitude to Senator Eugene J. McCarthy of Minnesota, who graciously undertook to write the Foreword for this study. Through ten years in the House of Representatives, and recently in the Senate, he has shown a scholarly grasp of the science of politics. His kinship with the tradition and spirit of the first Maryland assemblymen makes his reflections on their story a valuable contribution to the author's own purposes in these pages.

The encouragement and suggestion of Monsignor John Tracy Ellis regarding the present publication is gratefully acknowledged on this occasion. While the errors in fact and judgment are the author's, he would like to express his thanks for observations on his research by Lester J. Cappon, director of the Institute of Early American History and Culture, and for the editing and publishing of part of this study by Percy V. Norwood of Northwestern University, editor of *Church History*.

The author is grateful to his aunt, Miss Kathleen M. O'Brien, for her help with copy and the index. He would also like to express his appreciation to his students at Marquette University, who provided him with an image of the general reader for whom he has adapted his research.

CORRIGENDA

The following parts of lines on the original pages indicated should be corrected to read as given here:

P. 4, lines 1-2:   "prevailed over the assembly's determination."

P. 37, line 15:   "1588."

P. 55, Line 34:   *"Fide."*

P. 78, line 24:   "Englishmen [*angli*]."

P. 80, line 13:   "March 25."

P. 89, line 5:   "January 26."

P. 94, line 18:   "composed in 1639."

P. 97, line 22:   "what could have happened."

P. 97, line 29:   "could have made in a compromise."

P. 97, line 32:   "such actions as."

P. 113, line 33:   "after the ordinance, Puritans."

CONTENTS

xviii CONTENTS

THEIR RIGHTS AND LIBERTIES

*The Beginnings of Religious and Political
Freedom in Maryland*

INTRODUCTION

THE FIRST colonists of Maryland were intent upon political activity. This was so from their first moments in the New World. The hatches of the *Ark* and *Dove* had disgorged the motley sum of the Marylanders' worldly possessions. The bedraggled human cargo, four months in passage from England, hardly had become accustomed to firm land, when this unlikely group of men organized a political assembly. We have no written record of this first Maryland Assembly and learn of its existence only from asides that appear in the official minutes of the succeeding sessions. The dramatic movement of these subsequent sessions makes us certain that something more than sparks of interest in the affairs of state touched the shores of Maryland in March, 1634.

With unbelievable swiftness, events in Maryland within five years moved to a climax. The Proprietor of Maryland, Cecil Calvert, resided in England, secure in the potential power over the colony by virtue of the broad phrases of the charter which his father, George Calvert, first Lord Baltimore, had won from Charles I. But in the fresh, free atmosphere of the New World, the first colonists struck out boldly on a political course inspired more by this new freedom and the remembrance of English political traditions than by the letter of the Maryland Charter. The first Maryland assemblymen initiated legislation, and this challenged the proprietor. Calvert drafted his own code of laws, urging approval by the assembly in 1638. Under the leadership of a Captain Cornwallis, and in opposition to Leonard Calvert, resident Governor of Maryland, the assemblymen stood by their claim that they had the right to initiate legislation.

After failing to adjust a compromise, Lord Baltimore acquiesced in the assembly's determination to draft its own laws. The Maryland Ordinance of 1639 embodied what the assemblymen agreed should be the basic set of laws for the new colony and their understanding substantially differed from Baltimore's mind in the matter. As Governor Leonard Calvert admitted to his brother, the proprietor, concerning his code: "There were so many things unsuitable to the people's good."[1]

Surely the vital beginnings of self-government were to "the people's good." The era saw monarchs arbitrarily barter with the sacred rights of their subjects, and it was one of the hopes of the New World that it would protect its future citizens from this menace. As American colonial history unfolds, it proves a dramatic march toward democracy. A critical stage in the march was the growth of power in the representative assemblies of the colonies and their conflict with the crown, proprietor, and governor, who were the substance of potential monarchical tyranny. Herbert L. Osgood, a time-honored scholar of colonial America's political institutions, once concluded: "It is through a broad and thorough study of this conflict that we shall discover the main trend of events within the provinces themselves, and at the same time note the preparation of forces which were largely to occasion the revolt of 1776."[2]

The ordinance of 1639 as a chapter in the Maryland episode of this great historical movement holds claim to importance on additional grounds to that of self-government. A tradition of toleration was planted in the colony, and its roots were the measures of 1639. The autonomous nature of church and state became a dramatic issue in the ordinance and proved the underpinning of the practices of toleration which fostered this tradition from the beginning. In the march of events through 1776 toward the Constitutional Convention, added significance is given to the ordinance by the role that Maryland played in the Bill of Rights.

Marylander Daniel Carroll was among those who fashioned the First Amendment, the foundation of our religious liberty.

Though the society of early Maryland could hardly have been simpler, the force of early events on later developments was complex and as far reaching as we have suggested. The same is true of the influence of circumstances on the lives and thoughts of the first Maryland assemblymen. The story of these days can be told from the sources that remain; but to penetrate the struggle that persisted beneath demands analysis and recognition of broader historical movements. In meeting such a challenge, I have modestly concerned myself with a significant aspect of this whole and have brought a study to focus by consideration of the fact that the majority of the first Maryland assemblymen were Catholics.

To see what the understandings of the ordinance and early legislation demanded of these Catholics and the tradition to which their thought belonged seems a profitable study. For here we have the beginnings of a political tradition, rooted in England and modified by the New World. Even more, this is a human story of aspiration, struggle, and adjustment which we better understand by probing the thoughts of those who were its living characters. In this respect my study is not exclusive, nor at all points conclusive, in its consideration of the ordinance of 1639. Likewise, I hope to create an understanding of a group and a tradition rather than solve the many problems individuals pose. There were, too, other groups and different traditions at work in the Maryland historical process. It is my hope that in pursuing my primary purpose, light will be shed on these other considerations which individually deserve special study.

In understanding the men of the first Maryland Assembly, we are driven to investigate their experiences in England and the traditions which they brought with them to the New World. A salient feature of this background emerges in terms of relationships between church and state. What was the nature of the church, what was the nature of the state? Implicitly these questions arose from the time of Thomas More to the moment when George Calvert himself became involved with the Catholics in their striving for a *modus vivendi* under the English royal government. A train of agonizing events refined concepts of political as well as spiritual authority, for both intertwined in the fabric which delineates the growth of democracy. It is for this reason that church-state matters seem so important to the story. Vernon L. Parrington has done well in calling the colonial period a *theological age,* and for Maryland Catholics this was so even before their arrival in America.

From these various viewpoints, then—the growth of self-government, the distinction of church and state behind religious toleration, the interaction of religion and politics in the seventeenth century, and the fact of a Catholic majority in the first Maryland assemblies—we can grasp the fuller meaning of those experiences in early Maryland.

The current discussion of the nature of historical writing has called attention to the role of contemporary events and conditions in the outlook of the historian investigating the past. Surely the ancient historian Eusebius would not resent the scholar Lebreton of our day putting his hand to the retelling of the story of the primitive church. Whoever he be, the writer of a later date has at his disposal a knowledge derived from the years and from scholars hidden and celebrated; even if he only retells without any added wisdom a story suited to the hearing of his own day he has done a good thing. We can today view a maturing America and look back at one facet of its nursling existence—at its Catholic segment in Maryland. Since the time the Jesuit missionary, Father Andrew White, wrote his *Relation of 1634* in the primitive sanctuary of religious liberty off a cove of the Potomac, the scholarshsip on church and state and religious freedom has made it possible to tell the grandeur of those simple events White so humbly narrated. We can see the providential course of both secular and sacred history toward an America beneficial to the spouse of Christ, his Church, to whom Father White had dedicated himself as a priest and a missionary. The light of years makes it doubly rewarding to reread the narration of these beginnings.

Yet the spouse of Christ is a mystery, being as she is the extension in time of the divine life of the Eternal Word. Our concepts of this Church are veiled with the necessity of time as well as a divine obscurity. However, Catholic theology under the divine guidance promised the Church can deepen through the years its human insight. The state even more so has yielded up greater light as to its nature; and this not merely by accumulated study, but, as with the Church, out of the agony of human events. In this human experience and contemplation religious freedom is known and found to be a means of divine fulfillment.

Roger Williams, the founder of Rhode Island, once colorfully previewed one of his tracts with the title, *The Bloody Tenant of Persecution for cause of Conscience discussed in a Conference between Truth and Peace.* The general reader of our own day is introduced to the contents of a book in the less imaginative manner of the Introduction. He would not, perhaps, be attracted to the diffuse, scriptural case which Williams makes in his tract, the way a seventeenth-century New Englander was. He has, however, shown great interest in books about America's past, particularly when the narrative feature is generously employed and sufficient background is provided. For this reason I have kept the general reader in mind by using such a manner of presentation. Analysis, interpretation, and documentation may not always serve his interests as well; but they need not detract, since such elements give a deeper insight into the causes and significance of what the Marylanders were experiencing. The dominant movement of the whole story is the quest of these characters for "all their rights and liberties," something that appeals to men of all periods of history.

I. GOD'S SERVANT FIRST

HISTORIANS of colonial America have attached great importance to the events which were recorded in the proceedings of the first Maryland assemblies. Assumption of the power to initiate legislation, for example, has been put in the context of growth toward American independence.[1] Little noticed, however, is the distinction between church and state which we find in the Maryland ordinance passed by the assembly in 1639.[2] In an age of national religions, this is striking enough; but when we see the birth of religious toleration in the First Amendment of the Constitution of the United States and the role which Maryland played in this development in thought, the action of the Maryland assemblymen of that year takes on considerable historical importance. Toleration is a practice, and its practice is limited or expanded according to how one understands the state and its legitimate scope and the church as well.[3]

The more thorough histories of the American colonies do not neglect the background of those first events in Maryland and the men who provided the leadership for them. Many historians reach back more than a century to Thomas More, Lord Chancellor of Henry VIII.[4] Some connect him with Maryland through his great-grandson, Henry More, who made an important church-state settlement with Cecil Calvert in his disputes with the Jesuits. David Mathew, in his *Catholicism in England,* gives significant foundation for a direct influence in his portrait of the Catholic minority, its culture and tradition, from which the Maryland leadership was drawn.

"St. Thomas More," Mathew explains, "particularly by his life of defense, his prose style, and his personal legend, encouraged the families of the ancient Faith in their perseverance." As a hero, More's ideals influenced the average layman for many generations, since he, too, was compelled to think about problems of church and state in the face of the Elizabethan penal laws and Stuart oaths. Mathew seems to establish More as a monumental landmark, for he explains that the old religion "had preserved the old medieval traditions and was to gather those of St. Thomas More."[5] Biographers of More take a similar view, emphasizing his triple role as a literary, political, and ecclesiastical figure.[6]

The political scientist, from a different viewpoint, moves toward this same conclusion. The political events of the sixteenth century are admittedly difficult to interpret, but, as one writer remarks, "All we learn, and this is a great deal, is a most various questioning of old assumptions and all kinds of new beginnings which are going to make possible a theory of the state in the next century."[7] We can observe in the development of English thought a continuity which stretches from More through Cardinal Allen to the times of the Calverts. It proceeds along two lines, the personal right of conscience and the institutional right of the church; what More had to say on these two points was elaborated by those who came after him in the circumstances in which they found themselves.[8] The international character of the church, which all accepted, would be destroyed, More reasoned, if Henry usurped the spiritual authority of that body; it was in this way that the right of the king was limited by the right of the church and the nature of the civil authority defined. This conception of the state and church implied freedom for members of the church, but More made a more direct conclusion to personal rights and freedom of conscience. He saw provision for religious freedom in what were generally designated the rights of Englishmen. These rights in turn had roots in the very nature of man and the eternity of law itself and were the foundations for ramifications in com-

mon law and positive law. Whatever Henry VIII's deference to
Parliament, More saw that he was propelling England along the
course of absolutism; and by his resistance, More was enkindling
a flame of freedom which, fanned by others, would brighten a
better day.

So it is that when we read in the Maryland Ordinance of 1639
that "Holy Church within this province shall have all her rights
and privileges . . . [And the] Inhabitants of this Province shall
have all their rights and liberties according to the Great Charter
of England,"⁹ our minds turn back to Henry VIII's chancellor.
Like More, the Marylanders were in the shadow of a giant monarch and his proprietor; but, at the same time, we can see their
own kinship with ancient giants among the nobility in whose
presence John Lackland signed the Great Charter at Runnymede.

THOMAS MORE AND TUDOR KINGS

If the Marylanders were living in an era of divine right kings,
More's day was creating such kings. Monarchs were striving to
establish themselves over their nobility and to excel among their
fellow princes. The spirit of this contest is reflected with all its
naked force in the writings of Machiavelli when he said: "There
are two ways of contending—one in accordance with the laws, the
other by force; the first of which is proper to men, the second to
beasts. But since the first method is often ineffectual, it becomes
necessary to resort to the second." In this blend of sop to principle
and spur to expediency, the spokesman for the new order discussed practical examples for imitation. Cesare Borgia is described
in his pursuit of Romagna.¹⁰

More could have supplied Machiavelli with further examples.
He had written his life of Richard III about the time *The Prince*
was published. Richard, Duke of Gloucester, was in the pattern.
Cruel and cynical, he used his position as guardian of Edward
IV's will to initiate a train of events which put Edward V in the

Tower of London to face death; made himself suitor of his niece, heiress to the throne; and wrung from Parliament legal camouflage for his shameless conspiracy. Unlike Machiavelli, More is indignant at such a career and Bosworth Field is a judgment of justice. In his life of Richard III, More is sounding the alarm for the defense of English institutions against arbitrary and amoral politics.

When Henry, Earl of Richmond, triumphed over Richard at Bosworth Field in 1485 and became Henry VII, the trend of absolutism and the ideals of *The Prince* were not demolished. Henry took judicial power into his own hands by establishing the Star Chamber and by initiating a financial system open to the same arbitrary control. The situation was hardly conducive to a government which More approved, particularly in the military expenditures and expensive diplomacy involved in extending the Tudor family's power. William Roper, one of More's first biographers, tells us of an instance when Parliament successfully resisted Henry, More playing a prominent role in the opposition. The amount the king originally had asked for the marriage of his daughter Margaret to the king of Scotland was ninety pounds, but Parliament would settle for only forty. When a member of the king's privy chamber told Henry VII that "a beardless boy [More] had disappointed all his purpose," the king sought revenge. It was More's father who paid, to the amount of one hundred pounds on a charge contrived for the occasion. This was an omen, however exaggerated by Roper, of things to come.[11]

More's rise in public life brought him rather swiftly to the side of Henry VII's son. Before coming to the House of Commons, where he was at one time Speaker, More had been under-sheriff of London and chancellor of the Duchy of Lancaster. He had legal background in his father, who was judge of the king's bench, as well as in his own professional training. From privy councilor he came at the age of forty to the office of master of requests and finally served as lord chancellor of England. His

own attractive integrity and the modesty with which he wore his
learning won him the personal influence that did not necessarily
go with a position near the throne. Henry VIII forgot More as
the author-critic of absolutism and the defender of Parliament, if
he ever understood the mind of More in these matters; and we
see Henry promenade arm in arm with More in an English garden discussing matters of state.

Ironically, one of More's first disagreements with Henry derived from More's severer attitude toward the church. Julius II
was in the process of extending the Papal States in the direction
of Romagna and was relying on the League of Cambrai to rally
what princes he could against Louis XII of France, who opposed
this policy. Henry's extravagant cooperation in the League did
not win the sympathy of More. To Henry's reasoning that a
Christian prince should defend the vicar of Christ, More made
his own profound argument, which too few in his day appreciated. The league was subserving the temporal interests of the
papacy and, many might reason, the interests of the Rovere
family from which Julius came. More could recall that the papacy
had only recently served the interests of the Borgias in the person
of Rodrigo, Pope Alexander VI. In a sarcastic allusion to the
Roman emperors, Colet had warned against this situation where
one would render service to the worldly fortunes of Alexander
and Julius, which was apparently the light in which More saw
the project. Submission to the ancient spiritual authority did not
compel concurrence in political leagues for the temporal advantage of one who bore that inheritance.

The substance of this disagreement and the depth of More's
perception of the times emerged more fully when Henry VIII
presented him with his treatise, *Assertion of the Seven Sacraments,*
which was an answer to Luther's *Babylonian Captivity.* "I must
put your Highness in remembrance of one thing," More warned.
"The pope, as your Grace knoweth, is a prince as you are, and in

league with all [*sic*] other Christian princes. It may hereafter so
fall out that your Grace and he may vary upon some points of the
league, whereupon may grow breach of amity and war between
you both." More objected to Henry's determination to "set forth
that [papal] authority to the uttermost." He wished papal authority "more slenderly touched," calling attention to the temporal
nature of the papal action as distinct from the spiritual essence
of papal authority.[12] Henry, on the contrary, believed he had
in some way received his own temporal crown from papal authority. Subsequent events later proved how far Henry always
was from More in his conception not only of the church but of
the state as well. "Henry devoted the first half of his reign," says
Chambers of the irony of these events, "to promoting the interest
of the 'small Italian princedom,' and the second to destroying the
spiritual primacy."[13]

Obviously, More did not lay down his life for Henry's concept of the church and the papacy. At the same time we should
get the full picture of More in connection with Henry's *Assertion*. More was a humanist, bent on putting an end to selfish
dynastic wars; and he was an advisor of a king, not an equal, reserved in offering contrary advice. It remains to other circumstances of his life to describe his theology and philosophy which
he dramatized by his martyrdom. From his correspondence with
Cromwell, however, we do know that the occasion of his advice
on Henry's *Assertion* moved his thought in a direction of extreme
divergence from the King's view of church and state.[14]

Divergent views brought open conflict when Henry VIII thrust
the "great business" of his divorce upon his advisor. In 1527,
Henry appealed to Rome for a nullification of his marriage to
Catherine of Aragon, basing his case on the fact that she was the
widow of his brother Arthur and incapable for this reason of
being bound to him in matrimony. Desirous of making Anne
Boleyn his wife, he became dissatisfied with the scruples of

Wolsey and the delay in getting papal approval, with the result that he dismissed Wolsey in 1529 in favor of More. Because More felt bound in conscience to submit to the pope regarding the validity of the sacrament of matrimony in Henry's marriage to Catherine, his position as lord chancellor became impossible as the question took on increasing importance and attention.

In this position More further clarified the nature of the disagreement in thought which appeared earlier in connection with Henry's response to Luther. Henry posed not merely a theoretical question now, but a matter of civil obedience, which hinged on the nature and scope of church and state. More was careful in the way in which he refused approval of the divorce, so that he gave "no occasion of slander, of tumult and sedition" by any public discussion of the "great business." Although Henry could not make a case of treason against More for this reason, he nonetheless tried to put the matter of withheld consent on the grounds of civil disobedience. To More this was a matter of the state reaching into the realm of the spirit and belief. "Ye must understand," More simply explained, "that, in things touching conscience, every true and good subject is more bound to have respect to his said conscience and to his soul than to any other . . . in all the world. . . ."[15]

More resigned his office of Chancellor in 1532 and after two years was again brought into dispute for refusing approval of Henry's Act of Supremacy. In the series of questionings following his arrest, More with all his wit and gentleman's irony challenged his inquisitors with one fundamental question: must one serve men or God? On one point he made a more formal statement of his frame of mind:

Forasmuch as this indictment is grounded upon an Act of Parliament directly repugnant to the laws of God and His holy Church, the supreme government of which, or of any part whereof, may no temporal prince presume by any law to take upon him, as rightfully belonging to the See of Rome . . . ; it is therefore, in law amongst Christian men insufficient to charge any Christian man.[16]

Henry, as a Christian, was under the spiritual jurisdiction of the pope, More was saying; and in the very nature of things, he could not as head of the state take such jurisdiction to himself in a spiritual matter, however violently he might try. In presuming to do so, he distorted not only the nature of the state but of the church as well; and he was violating English law in its written and traditional provision for the rights of the church. More thrust the consequences of these usurpations upon his interrogators with such questions as, what will become of the universality of Christendom if each prince is free to determine that belief which is the basis of its historic unity? What limit is there to royal power? Few faced these questions immediately and fewer understood them as More did; but ultimately all would experience the consequence of these decisions.

Anyone who has made the charming acquaintance of More in his biography will expect him to speak out in his own distinctive manner on how he judged this crisis in history which he lived within his own soul. In view of More's personality, it is understandable that he did not finish his projected study which began with Richard III, but turned instead to *Utopia*. The imaginative cast of reality, which he so much admired in the Greek classics, was not to be expressed in regal biography. Nor do we feel that he is himself as he writes his *Apology*: apologetics is necessarily tedious, and circumstances alone drove him to it. Understandably, some see a change of character in him as he speaks in his *Apology* of heresy, monasticism, and other topics in the explosive context of European society. Some of these critics of the More delineated in the *Apology* turn to *Utopia* for security in the friendship that More seems to win from those who follow the course of his life. Undoubtedly, they say of *Utopia,* this is More. If he must argue against capital punishment for thieves, he chooses the Platonic dialogue as a pleasant means to present his views. In so developing the first book of *Utopia,* More gets down to many serious matters; but, as with the business of beheading, it is his bent always to conduct the discussion with a generous measure of humor and imagination. More satisfies his humanist's flair by making the New World the locale of his business at hand. Hythloday, a traveler of the world and recently returned from America, is the fascinating medium of a report on a strange new way of life in which More artistically reflects on the trend of events and institutions in Europe.

More was no multiple-advocate; otherwise, he would have written a *Utopia* according to the current meaning of that word. He is constructing no Brave New World but trying to hold on to the old where he finds something firm enough to grasp; he is too humble and modest to sketch a blueprint for a New Harmony. One must be reasonable and imaginative, rather than merely emotional, to receive the message of Hythloday. *Utopia* is an *a fortiori* insinuation, which touches the pride of Englishmen; it has a gentle touch and is More's own adaptation of the role of the gadfly in the Greek philosopher, yet constructive and conservative, more pleasant in its effect than the grim *Crito.* His case rests upon a judgment reached rather by principles than by comparison to an ideally contrived society. For this he must be labeled a political philosopher, but again he will philosophize in his own mood, which is not that of Plato's *Republic.* If the advocate is tedious, the political philosopher can be soporific in his definitions, formulations, and keenly felt responsibility to the letter of his written expression. Because all of this was not congenial to More, the book that seemed his delight had none of it. Instead, we must learn to see that what he is not advocating as a practice, he is describing to suggest a principle. Only in this way does he rise above the tedium of the advocate and the boredom of the philosopher in presenting the principles which emerge in response to the society in which he was tragically immersed.

More's philosophical principles have been misunderstood by many because they have not known him as a person and in terms of this device of *Utopia* by which he chose to express himself. It can be reasonably objected, however, that More's philosophy would seem better revealed in his direct philosophizing, in the pages of his *Apology,* for example. Yet, the *Apology* says too much of the circumstances in England to the eventual confusion of principles, and it befuddles the mind that would understand More's premises. This was particularly the danger in the period of great transition in England in which More lived. The course of events stimulated reflection on principles, but individuals were plainly at a loss to perceive how they applied to the complicated circumstances in sixteenth-century England which demanded solutions. The device of *Utopia* lifted the principles of More out of these complexities and simply delineated them in the uncomplicated society of the Utopians.[17] In doing this he enabled us to see what he held, how he was inevitably at odds with the trend toward absolutism, and why his thought was related to the rise of a church-state view which established the autonomy and rights of each.

The worth of human nature, its integrity and potential, persisted in the thought and writing of More, as in the other humanists of his day. It logically led to optimistic conclusions about the nature of the state, its soundness, and hence its autonomy. In More's own day could be found those who, having misread Augustine, thought that the fall of man by original sin alone gave rise to the state. Passages of Augustine doubtlessly can be made to mean suspicion and even pessimism regarding human nature. Augustine brooded profoundly on the mystery of man as a compound of spirit and matter. Luther, in the context of personal sin, and Calvin, in the face of inexorable predestination, brooded less profoundly and arrived at human depravity. With Augustine and other Fathers of the Church, however, it is not the state as such that is related to sin, but one of its several functions which is the maintenance of civil peace and order; for the state originates from human nature itself and not its defects; this by virtue of the divine will of the Creator. "It was Luther," Messner observes, "who first abandoned the line of thought set out by St. Augustine and consigned the state wholly to the realm of sin and fallen nature."[18] More attacked Luther in common cause with his friend Erasmus who was alarmed at the destruction of free will by Luther. Certainly More could not stand to see man reduced to the dimensions portrayed in Machiavelli's treatise, an animal who is, from time to time, rational.

The prevailing climate of Nominalism hardly provided Luther the guidance necessary for a social philosophy. If anything, it drove him to a position of anti-intellectualism and low regard of human nature. In *Utopia* More attacked this decadent philosophy with youthful zest, particularly its over-used textbooks, the *logicales minores*. Utopian youths were not subjected to the barbarous niceties and pointless distinctions of these textbooks. The European traveler so trained could not make himself understood when he defined man in the abstract as common to all men in particular. Such a man was a colossus to the Utopian, even if the traveler pointed his finger at a man to make it clear about whom he was speaking.[19]

More positively identified himself with an Aristotelian-Thomistic tradition of intellectualism and the Schoolmen of an earlier day before the decline which Nominalism reflected. In his controversy with Luther, More used vigorous language to vindicate the Angelic Doctor, Thomas Aquinas. Once, speaking against Tyndale, he had commended the mingling of philosophy with theology. "This is a thing that may in place be very well done, since the wisdom of philosophy, all that we find true therein, is the wisdom given of God and may well do service to his other gifts of wisdom. . . ."[20] Here is the hallmark of man's integrity for More, the ability to philosophize in harmony with divine revelation. Original sin had not destroyed this possibility for Aquinas as it had for Luther and Calvin. That is why More found Aquinas congenial reading. Something of an eclectic, however, More drew from various medieval Schoolmen. Certainly he possessed no elaboration of Aquinas' political philosophy such as Bellarmine made in a succeeding generation. More held, nevertheless, a basic insight into man's nature which provided a valid foundation for the autonomy of the state and for democratic practices within it, a view later held by Bellarmine.

More moved very easily to his description of democratic foundations in *Utopia*. "Thirty families," he explained, "each choose a magistrate every year. . . . From among four men who are nominated by the people at large, they choose a king by secret ballot. . . . He rules for life unless he comes under suspicion of tyranny. . . ."[21] The significant point in these passages is not the provision for monarchy but the suppositions which controlled and modified it. The advantage of monarchy, as Aquinas had pointed out long before More, was the unity and leadership which it gave the state. This is essentially the notion of the executive features in democratic governments. The Utopian provision for popular will in the choice of the king challenged absolutism and royal inheritance in the structure of the state. There were absolutists who said that the king's authority was derived from his subjects, but their supposition was quite different from More's. Not the consent of his subjects but their chaotic nature and its need for a master confirmed the divine wisdom of absolute kingship. The king alone by his force could save the people from themselves, as Machiavelli would have described this issue. More, on the contrary, implied a far more wholesome esteem of human nature in rejecting inherited rule and relying on the consent of subjects. The state and its rule were viewed as a perfection of man, an outward expression of his social nature which God created as good

and integral. More seems to have been speaking in terms of the
Thomistic view of human nature.[22]

Again, in the state's dealing with religious matters, More's view
of man and his destiny becomes important. He stated that non-
Christians in Utopia were able to acquire a certain minimum
knowledge of God and the principles which underlie public morality. The Christian practiced religion and morality on a higher
supernatural level which the kingdom of God had created; yet
pagans may win celestial citizenship even though they seemed
to die pagans. Supposing that they could not explicitly accept
Christianity with sincerity, they still could live according to their
conscience as enlightened by the essential truths so widely held in
Utopia. Here More was reflecting a well-known theological view
that God's providence somehow supplies the supernatural element
needed for salvation. Luther would have said that the pagan must
accept Christ by saving faith; Calvin would have come to a more
pessimistic judgment from his theory of predestination.[23]

Against this hopeful background of the economy of salvation
as expressed in the case of the pagan, More's reader was not
scandalized when he read that magistrates of Utopia did not suppress heresy in the European manner. Public peace in the temporal
order alone seemed to be the concern of the magistrate *qua* magistrate. It is true that Utopians feared that without religion public
morality would not stand. Belief in a Supreme Being was given
public approval, although individuals were not compelled to share
this belief. With the European in mind, *Utopia* explained: "If
one religion alone be true and the others false, it will then easily
show itself so, provided it is advanced with reason and restraint,
as it emerges by the force of truth alone. . . ." The visitor to
Utopia observed the results of such a policy. "Those who do not
accept the Christian religion," he explained, "do not restrain others
from going over to it."[24]

There was, however, one report which tells how a Christian

was punished for speaking in public against other religions. "He was convicted and banished, not as a scorner of religion, but for stirring up disorder among the people; for they consider this among their most ancient practices, that no one's religion should be an injury to him." Citizens were free to debate and propagate their beliefs, but always with proper regard for civil peace. The state's concern was with the civil aspect only; and in his *Apology,* as well as in his own conflict with the crown, More expressed this principle.[25]

While Henry VIII and other European monarchs defended the use of a strong hand in religious controversy on the grounds of public order, they tended to demand broader powers than these grounds required. There were before Henry's times laws for the punishment of heresy, and in their application these, no doubt, often abridged freedom of conscience. Determination of orthodoxy, however, was still in the hands of the bearers of spiritual authority. In the conflict in which More found himself, Henry had taken a bold stride to new ground which pretended to spiritual authority, thereby giving to the state the power directly to determine belief. The various articles to effect religious conformity followed in Henry's lifetime and became a feature of royal power thereafter. Protestants as well as Catholics were to experience the intolerance which inevitably flows from such a notion of the state and its power.

On this subject More, in the *Utopia,* distinguishes two principles: He forcefully rejects coercion of belief and affirms civil authority over the peace as affected by public expression of belief. Nowhere do we find the rulers of Utopia drafting articles of faith and acts of supremacy. We see instead a state circumscribed by its essentially temporal nature. This was the lesson England had to learn. More taught it to his times by the imagery of *Utopia.*[26] We cannot credit More with prophecy when we use events that took place after the writing of *Utopia* to illustrate what

the Utopian state opposed; but we do have an arresting instance
of his insights into the issues of his day.

POPE GELASIUS AND THOMAS MORE

There is a dignity given to the state within the temporal boundaries More marked out for it as proper to its nature. The temporal
common good is worthy enough to demand the entire attention of
King Utopus, for the temporal common good constitutes the
state's distinctive purpose. European monarchs were to dishonor
the state in reaching beyond the temporal boundaries into the
strictly spiritual order, as Henry did when beguiled by illusion and
ambition. Henry brought on a condition in which the church became a department of the state. On the other hand, the notion of
the state as the *secular arm* of the church was fraught with this
same twofold danger of illusion and ambition. Churchmen, by
usurping the temporal authority, could destroy religious liberty
and even make the state a department of the church. In this latter
tradition we find a Christian prince assuming responsibility for
preaching the Gospel; More's opposition to this tendency was an
echo of Alcuin, who once spoke to Charlemagne in an attempt to
deter him from violating the consciences of the Saxons. More actually lived to see the day when the prince would fix belief by
playing the role of defender of orthodoxy as well as benefactor of
the Gospel. In Utopia, on the other hand, the state did not need
to usurp responsibility for the spiritual goal of the church in order
to be worthy; and many events showed that such distortions of
the role of the state degraded the church. Utopia had given the
church freedom to preach the Gospel by the circumstances of justice and peace which civil government had created. Perhaps to
Henry VIII, the *Defender of the Faith* and *His Catholic Majesty*,
this was a minimum achievement, but it was a fundamental one,
the most immediate function of the state in relation to the church
and the religious life of the citizens.

Was not Utopia spiritualizing the church to the vanishing point, making it an institution for angels rather than men? More does give the church a realistic position in the area of mixed temporal and spiritual matters. This is largely effected by establishing the transcendence of the church, without compromising what he holds on the integrity of the state. The example More uses to make his point is the unworthy cleric who is guilty of a felony for which a layman would be imprisoned. Such a man is to be let alone. What about public order? Hythloday explains that priests are very carefully selected, and that the high caliber of religious life among the laity, from whom they are chosen, guarantees a uniformly worthy clergy. The single exception is punished by the reproach of his own conscience and the opinion of Utopians. The case, therefore, does not involve any public disorder, so the state does not have to act.

How does all this touch the problem of England where the clergy needed reform? More is not directly solving a problem but only influencing solutions; and he does so by making it clear that the state is not the keeper of the church, neither in Henry's nor in Philip's impersonation of that role. The church transcends the state in her goal and in the means of its achievement. Of this More leaves no doubt. If the spirit of Christ's poverty lags among the clergy, the church must use her own means of renewal and reform. If a king would not interfere with the luxury enjoyed by his citizens, why should he in the case of those who have an ecclesiastical status? Yet the context makes it clear that *Utopia* has not underwritten ecclesiastical license. If public peace did suffer any distress, More seems to imply that charges would be made and judgment rendered by a civil magistrate. How would he reconcile this with the system of ecclesiastical courts which kept the clergy from such magistrates? The best that we can say is that More would limit the scope of these courts. Immunity of the clergy and their special tribunals was an institution of gradual growth through a period dominated by feudalism. A conclusive and valid adjustment of values regarding this development in the face of the new structure of European society was entirely discerned neither by More nor anyone else of his day. What More was sure of, he made strikingly clear in *Utopia:* the church was an autonomous spiritual society transcending the temporal in some way similar to and yet distinct from the transcendence of the individual's personal destiny. This is the meaning we gather from the passage on the clergy and that on the freedom of the pagan. The church in *Utopia* benefits from the understanding of the state as distinctive in its temporal goal, in the pursuit of which, like the church, the state is autonomous. *Utopia* engenders the hope that a mutual respect by church and state will promote the advantage of the citizen in whom the two authorities converge, thus fulfilling the twofold destiny of man as a terrestrial and celestial citizen.

Utopia was written before More became chancellor and before he wrote the *Apology.* In the complicated circumstances in which the *Apology* settled church-state matters, it might appear that More had forgotten the Utopian vision of principles which we have just described, or that he had never actually accepted them. In his dealing with heresy, in particular, this difficulty comes forward and some have concluded that tolerant citizen More became the persecuting chancellor. There is less difficulty, however, with his controversial writing in the *Apology* than in his action as a magistrate for cases of heresy. In the former instance the personal invective of his adversaries and their reckless assault on persons and institutions justified his tactics.[27] Even here, his wit in the *reductio ad absurdum* has more of humor and less bitterness than one would expect in the situation.

To understand More as the magistrate, however, we must measure the office and the laws which were to be enforced by it against heretics. Perhaps the best starting point is the Peasants' Revolt of 1381. To the economic pressure which the shift away from the feudal status of the peasant was causing, there was added the ingredient of religious radicalism which John Wycliffe had sown. The preaching of the poor priests, as Wycliffe's leaders were called, was thus related to the public disorder of the Peasants' Revolt. It was this fact which alienated Wycliffe from the educated minds of England. The laws against spreading theological innovations which followed carried the connotation of the Revolt. These were the laws that More was to enforce. It is indeed conceivable that one could see in them, as More seemed to, measures necessary for the temporal good of the realm. This understanding is compatible with the account in *Utopia* of penalties against one "inflaming the people to sedition" by preaching on the Christian religion. More's *Apology* makes a good deal of the issue of public peace in these matters.[28] Undoubtedly More was concerned about the spiritual consequences among the populace of the preaching of heresy, but it is not certain that he believed it his concern *as magistrate*. The temptation to assume responsibility for the religious orthodoxy of his citizens would be more easily resisted in a pluralistic society, since a greater presumption of sincerity could be made in favor of one not holding the traditional beliefs.

In light of all of these considerations we can begin to see that More would have been at home in Maryland. Such a pluralistic society was unknown to him, but the principles of adjustment were not. The thought development which would take place from the starting point which he had constructed would prove More's kinship with Maryland.

As a starting point of a development which carried thought through a period of historical transition, did More launch forth unencumbered by the baggage of tradition? Or was he a conservative, resisting dangerous trends?

More is unmistakably a conservative in his appeal to the past and to established institutions, but he was by force of circumstances compelled to be something more than this. The Tudors also made strong appeals to the conservative mind. They had argued the need of obeying God in the civil ruler who must be strong if he would tame the perverse inclinations of men and remedy the disorder of society which had found place even in the church. The framework of this tradition of conservatism, however, was being greatly modified. Feudalism was declining and with it the exactness of those understandings which centered in the notion of the *Respublica Christiana,* with the result that the church declined and the state assumed a wider role in the social lives of men. In the adjustment, inherited diversity of opinion regarding the nature of the church and the state came into application. More had to take a stand where there was divergence among medieval thinkers in these matters and, in the crucible of the peculiar circumstances of his own day, arrive at deeper insights to guide him. His conclusions might differ from custom and leave him a liberal by description,[29] but he was making his way as a conservative under the initial influence of traditional principles.

In the discussion of church-state relations throughout the centuries we find creative thinkers returning to a center of gravity such as More had described in *Utopia.* The two distinct orders in Utopian society were reminiscent of the remarkable formulation of Pope Gelasius in A.D. 494. In the many quests for balance in church-state relations through the Middle Ages, Gelasius was quoted, and at times misinterpreted, by those who were locked either theoretically or practically in a church-state impasse. "There are indeed . . . two powers," Gelasius said, "by which this world is chiefly ruled: the sacred power of the popes and the royal power." Even in this limited form, distinction and separation seem clear. Gelasius told the emperor, to whom these words were addressed, "You must submit yourself faithfully to those who have charge of divine things, and look to them for the means of your salvation."[30] It cannot be inferred from this statement that Gelasius wished to put the imperial power at the disposal of the church.

The circumstances in which Gelasius wrote his admonition to

the Emperor Anastasius I were somewhat similar to those More found in Europe in his day and which would soon develop in England. The Arians dominated the Italian peninsula, depriving Gelasius of the benefits he might have enjoyed as pope during the earlier period when his church was the official religion of the Empire. In the Eastern Empire, to which he addressed his letter, this official status continued and led to the embarrassment which occasioned the letter. Anastasius was interfering in the appointment of bishops and was instrumental in heretics taking ecclesiastical offices. In criticizing this extreme swing of the pendulum, Gelasius did advance a position at the other extreme: "For if in matters pertaining to the administration of public discipline, the bishops of the church, knowing the empire has been conferred on you by divine instrumentality, are themselves obedient to your laws, lest in purely material matters contrary opinions may seem to be voiced, with what willingness, I ask you, should you obey those to whom is assigned the administration of divine mysteries."[31] In these words Gelasius accepted the real possibility of officials of the church failing to comply with civil authority and not merely the usurpation in which Anastasius indulged. The situation in Italy had helped the church at least in that the civil ruler could not by any official tie with the church presume to activities such as Gelasius criticized in Anastasius. The pope from this position could discern much better the distinction of each order. In somewhat the same way Catholics who followed More would be driven to a similar insight, but they were also driven to an understanding of the limits of the state as a result of a discrimination which was not experienced by Gelasius at the time that he wrote his letter.

It might be observed that Gelasius, for all the preciseness of his formula, did not entirely determine a course in mixed matters of church and state, where the line between temporal and spiritual is not clear. Erastians did, as a matter of fact, use Gelasius to refute Gelasius in the mouth of his successors. From our disinterested historical position, we might in these instances of mixed matters show that his formula did apply even though contemporaries erred through inherent limitations of the times or through their own lack of sincerity. Beyond this we can supply a realistic element to the two powers formulation from the writings of Gelasius himself.

In his *Fourth Tractate,* Gelasius introduced a consideration of human frailty which had considerable influence on the application of this formulation. He explained that before the coming of Christ, royal and priestly power were often combined in the same person, according to the Old Testament. But in the New Testament we see that Christ does not take to himself any temporal power. Gelasius further enforced the notion of distinction of powers by stating that the supernatural order established by Christ and his revelation had not changed the fact, even though the Old Testament times were under a different dispensation. The great lesson of a Christ without a temporal rule was then stated: "Christ being mindful of human frailty and the welfare of his followers . . . decreed that the power of each office be distinct from the other in both function and dignity, thus protecting humility and avoiding pride. . . ."[32] This statement injected a guiding spirit into the formulation which Gelasius sent to Anastasius, one which engenders a reticence on the part of both church and state in dealing with each other. There was no oversimplification which destroyed a functional cooperation between church and state to the advantage of the citizen. At the same time cooperation was safeguarded by an awareness that there is a tendency to usurp, a tendency of that human frailty which both prince and prelate bore in his person. The implication would be that reserve in the exercise of power on both sides was more prudent in a case of doubt.

This very reserve, which reveals its respect of church and state for each other, as well as a prudent estimate of human frailty, characterized the relations outlined in *Utopia.* The state, if it errs, does so on the side of restraint when it deals with the clergyman who could be arrested; the church, if lenient, supports the state and its role of promoting the temporal good and religious freedom of its citizens whether pagan or Christian.

The whole force of events in More's lifetime, and in the era which preceded it, drove him toward a Gelasian understanding of the spiritual society as distinct from the temporal. All about him, More had seen from his earliest days churchmen bedecking themselves with the luxury of worldly princes, politicizing outside their own circle, their offices the prize political plums among secular rulers. He also saw the teachings of Marsilius of Padua and John Wycliffe which were born of such conditions.[33] Both men advanced theories that would ultimately lead not only to a denial of the necessary temporal circumstances of the church, but even of a visible form. This radicalism had in More's day reached only the point where the civil ruler and his pliant bishops intended to control the temporal circumstances of the church, as the tradition of Marsilian thought provided. The memory of the Council of Constance was yet fresh, that landmark of restored church unity, in which Sigismund, the Holy Roman Emperor, played such an important role. Splintered by pope and anti-pope, the spiritual society seemed on the verge of destruction when a temporal prince by his force and prestige convened the Council in 1414.

The monarchs of the sixteenth century gave their own meaning and application of this tradition in the circumstances of the national states. Philip was "His Catholic Majesty," Henry, "Defender of the Faith," French rulers inherited the appellation, "His Christian Majesty." Philip II was carried away by his role in the church as he had been taught to understand it. The Spanish Inquisition expressed his own enthusiasm as well as the mentality of the day. Most significantly, Philip did not permit cases before this body to be appealed to Rome; and he hesitated to allow the

decrees of the Council of Trent to be read in his country,[34] seem-
ingly regarding them as the acts of usurpation.

The convergence of this line of thought on the rise of the national state created the state religions of modern times. Charles V
revealed the influence of these concurrent forces in his life when
he laid his mighty sceptre in the hands of his son, Philip II.
"Above all," he tells his people, "beware of the infection from the
sects of neighboring lands. Extirpate at once the germs of heresy,
should they appear in your midst, for fear lest they may spread
abroad and utterly ruin your state, and lest you fall into the direst
calamities."[35] Like a medieval prince, he professes devotion to the
role of protector of his people, especially in regard to their spiritual welfare. As a king of modern Europe, however, the religious
beliefs of his rival princes were not the same as his own, and he
foresaw that they might sow this discord among his own subjects
in order to prepare for his overthrow. The upshot of this infer-
ence, particularly in England and Spain, was to make religious
conformity synonymous with patriotism when the monarch was
hard pressed by his foes.

These royal custodians appeared in church-state relations in
reaction not only to a church in need of reform and to the new
pattern of national states, but to the temporal power of the popes
and the theoretical claims to it during the late Middle Ages. Ties
of citizenship to the temporal prince were tenuous during the
Middle Ages by the very nature of feudalism. The church was
even visibly more evident than the state. Innocent III's contest
with the King of England illustrated this. Europe, indeed, was
conceived as a *Respublica Christiana,* a Christian republic, which
created a political unity, even if on a religious basis, where feudalism provided none. Some Europeans came to think of the pontiff
as the source from which all authority radiated, both civil and
ecclesiastical, even if a theologian such as Aquinas may have defined things otherwise in keeping with the Gelasian tradition.
The church in official teaching often returned to the thought of

Gelasius when it stated that Christ had foregone temporal authority and its origin could not be traced to his successors. Yet Boni-
face VIII in the same period spoke in terms which eventually
elicited a counter challenge at the other extreme—a state absorbing the church instead of a church absorbing a state.

Henry VIII, by what he said against Luther in his *Assertion of
the Seven Sacraments,* by his policy on the League of Cambrai,
and by the tragic conflict with More, revealed that confusion of
mind on the nature of church and state which was so characteristic of the late Middle Ages. More's advocacy of the Gelasian
formula in these circumstances as well as in *Utopia* could not be
described as beacon lights over the troubled waters; but surely his
own enlightenment was to contribute to the growth of a tradition
which would make for a better day in the New World. But More's
enlightenment was lost on Henry VIII. Henry did not accept
the meaning of *Utopia,* nor did he seem to understand the consequences More put down as inevitable in the course the king had
chosen. Henry did not see, or did not care to see, destruction of
the universality of the church in the steps that he was taking.
What Christians believed, he reasoned, was common knowledge
and the king would never be forced by circumstances to fix its
meaning. Heresy abroad did not disturb him, since this was a
perennial phenomenon in the church's life. What he did not see
was that this common doctrine of Christendom became so through
an authoritatively teaching church. If unity were to continue, it
must have such a guiding voice. Cast adrift from Rome, Henry
himself was compelled to become that voice in the troubled waters
which all too soon swept about his national church. Things became politically and religiously urgent, for the Protestant evan-
gel was increasing its volume. In the circumstances the power of
the state expanded to proportions it had never known. Royal pressure had stifled the halls of Parliament; now it had entered the
sanctuary of religious liberty and dictated religious belief.

Events were all too soon to confirm the accuracy of More's understanding of these events. In 1534 the Act of Supremacy was accomplished, and the following year More died in opposition to it. Within five years Henry was driven to define theological dogma when the traditional teaching of the church came in question, the very role he had thought the crown would never play and the one which More had predicted was inevitable. The reign of Edward VI threw the doors open to the new theology, and Cranmer drafted the essentials of Anglicanism. Elizabeth later replaced these with the Thirty-nine Articles, which were calculated to win religious unity by blending Protestant dogma with traditional ritual; this she had hoped would create a religious unity capable of bolstering the national state. All was in vain, for the Puritan movement came into existence and began the harassment of Anglicanism which lasted for a century. Among the Catholic minority, More became with the passage of time a symbol and a legend; and its leaders grew to the stature of More's thought, even advancing by the force of events to a greater understanding of the nature of church and state.

II. THE KING'S GOOD SERVANTS

MORE's impeccable orthodoxy and fidelity to conscience in no way cooled his ardent patriotism. He did not raise his voice in the market place against the king's heterodox decision because Henry, in spite of his act of tyranny, was still the civil authority and the sacred symbol of the England that More loved. More had once implied that he would take the field with an English king against the pope himself were it a field of temporal conflict. He had said that he was "God's servant first," but he did not thereby deny loyalty to the king.

The intersecting of these two intense loyalties was the crux of More's tragedy. Its poignancy men of like loyalties must suffer when they are confronted with acts of tyranny or intolerance from either prince or prelate. Those who steered More's course of being both God's and the King's good servants in the years following More's death in 1635 were to undergo even greater trials, for international affairs and royal policy increasingly complicated the practices of patriotism and conscience. Conformists contrived circumstances which were calculated to establish an apparent conflict in the dual loyalty of Catholics. The papacy was made to appear essentially a temporal authority, thereby constituting a compromise in patriotism to those who professed obedience to it. Thomas More had done a merciful service to these souls in distress. He had shown them the limits of the temporal sovereign and branded subtle usurpations of spiritual authority by princes for what they were. This was the Catholic minority's counter-weapon in the immediate conflict with Tudor and Stuart monarchs.

There was, however, a constructive development of More's tradition made within the Catholic camp during this period. A deeper understanding of the spiritual nature of the church was arrived at, particularly by those English Catholics who would pursue church-state considerations in the New World. The applications that followed in Maryland had matured during the previous hundred years of anguish in the mother country following More's death.

CARDINAL ALLEN AND QUEEN ELIZABETH

It was during the reign of Edward VI that Englishmen came to understand the full import of his father's Act of Supremacy. Parliament had executed Anne Boleyn on a charge of adultery and, for the moment, thus disinherited her daughter Elizabeth. Edward, who was born of Henry's union with Jane Seymour, succeeded to the throne, passing over Mary, Henry's daughter by Catherine of Aragon, considered by him to be illegitimate. During Edward's reign Protestant theology spread throughout England. The boy's advisors had repealed the Six Articles of orthodox belief in 1547. By 1551 the crown, especially under Cranmer, had begun to gather the new doctrines together into what eventually became the Forty-two Articles of belief. Henry had already defined heresy and declared that the king had the power to judge belief; now the king of England had formulated belief with the great detail which created the Anglican religion. All along the temporal power of the crown implemented these decisions in spiritual matters and enforced conformity to them; for the state was not distinct from the church, and there was no political entity that would stand up for the rights of dissenting Englishmen, once effectively defended by the papacy.

With the spread of Protestantism, a pluralistic society was being created, so that Catholics lived with many different sects in addition to Anglicanism. The supposition had to be made that Protestants were sincere. The religion of the state had been vastly transformed in great detail, so that Catholics could not escape the fact of many substantial differences from their own creed.

This was a complicating development but it was not entirely an unfortunate one, as subsequent history reveals. Catholics examined their beliefs with greater fervor and sincerity and were freer from any deceitful compromises. Sincerity in the heretic opened the door to the reality of tolerance and those considerations which were found in *Utopia* to support it: the generation whose religion was a prey to cowardice in the face of persecution, and ambition in the face of royal favors for conformists, was leaving this world for the next. The minority sects which were taking root would join those Catholics who sought to limit the power of government. All of these religious forces had a subtle influence on the drift of events toward democratic government.

In the immediate struggle for survival and for the light to see their way, Catholics received a respite in the reign of Mary Tudor. The rule of Edward VI, who took the throne at the age of ten, was brief; his protector, the Duke of Northumberland, sought to steer the succession away from Elizabeth and Mary when the end of Edward's reign drew near in 1553. He supported the claim of Lady Jane Grey, cousin of Edward, and prevailed upon the king to assign the royal power to her. The marriage of Northumberland's son to Lady Jane indicated, however, a bid for power which turned Parliament and public favor away from Northumberland's scheme. It was in this way that the Roman Catholic Mary came to the throne and attempted to restore the beliefs which had unified England before the time of Henry VIII's break with Rome. Practices dear to Catholics were now permitted in public, and this instilled new confidence.

All was not blessing in the Catholic reign, however. "Mary's life," says Philip Hughes, "from the day when Henry VIII announced to her mother that he did not believe she was his wife—

when Mary was a child of eleven—down to the day, ten years later, when, after the death of her mother, he reduced her to signing an acknowledgment that she too did not believe it, was such that it is marvellous the adolescent girl came out of it with her reason. That these terrible years took their toll in physical and emotional ailments that were permanent is a matter of history. At thirty-seven she was already ageing."[1] Surely one could not look here for the sagacious leadership inspired by the wisdom which Thomas More bequeathed to the English Catholic's political tradition. Mary reached to Spain for the hand of Charles V to guide her first halting steps. This foreign dependence reached fulfillment in her marriage treaty with Charles' son, Philip II, King of Spain. It was not until three years later that the Englishman, Reginald Pole, became Archbishop of Canterbury, remote by then from any position of superior influence in the decisions of Mary.

Public resumption of Roman Catholic practices brought Protestant outcries and riots. If More had faced this situation as magistrate, he would have merely applied the long established laws against religious disturbers of the peace. Mary's purposes and policies went beyond this and were inspired by Philip II and his Spanish tradition rather than More and the common law of England. Special laws against heresy were applied and aided the effort to bring especially the non-Roman hierarchy into conformity. Listed among their victims was Cranmer, who died recanting at the stake. A Henrican conspiracy had overthrown the church and enslaved thousands of Catholics, some reasoned, and Mary was the liberator. But there was more than conspiracy. There was the fact of the new gospel and its increasing acceptance during the reign of Edward. There was sincerity of belief and a pluralistic society to deal with and no one equal to such a task. Could the king's counsellor, More, have discerned the application of those principles of toleration which he enunciated in his concepts of the church and state? Surely the author of *Utopia* would not have disregarded the reality of a pluralistic society with its implications for toleration. But the movement of such events as these was beyond one man and in point of time his tradition was too insufficiently formed to serve as a rudder to statecraft.

It was during the reign of Elizabeth that the thoughts of More began to mature. Conformists accused More of treason. The circumstances of the Spanish alliance created by Mary now seemed fertile ground to renew a case of treason against Catholics. The diplomatic contest with Spain which soon developed heightened the zest for prosecution. None had forgotten that England had lost Calais in France because of Spain. In commerce there had never been a community of interests between the two countries. An era of running battles between English "Sea Dogs" and Spanish galleons was an ominous prelude to the contest with the Spanish Armada in 1688. The Dutch concurred with the English as they saw that they must break the Spanish monopoly if each would fulfill its longings which were both mercenary and patriotic.

In this strenuous effort it was important to marshal every effort, and religion could not have been spared. What nation has not listed God as its first ally? In the wake of the division of Christendom, nations became synonymous with sect, particularly in the Anglo-Spanish cleavage, and this engendered bitter rivalries. An outgrowth of this situation was the pressure for religious conformity according to the national religion. Elizabeth instituted penal laws which compelled religious practices in conformity with her Thirty-nine Articles of belief. While the Puritan sectarians took issue with this creed, the chief minority was Catholic, and it was they who bore the hardship of penalties for adhering to their heterodox practices. To the mind of the times there must be a state religion; a people must be religiously united, even if minorities must suffer. And the conflict with Spain seemed to make it all the more inevitable and necessary.

We can perhaps best sense the anguish of the Catholic's conflict

and the complexity of church-state issues in Robert Persons. He
was English and trained in the Oxford tradition. He had tutored
at Baliol and in 1575, after coming under the influence of Father
Good, became a Jesuit. England wanted to be Catholic, he believed, and he would help bring her what she wished through the
vocation he had followed. Studying at Rome with this fired imagination he inspired the "oath of the missions," a long since honored religious practice of missionaries by which they solemnly
promise to serve God in a mission field. He served as Rector of
the English College in Rome, founded to train missionaries for
England. Within five years, Persons had directly made good his
oath, leading one of the first missionary bands into Elizabethan
England. Edmund Campion has immortalized this missionary
chapter as a brilliant Oxford don, honored by the Queen, and
dying the noble gentleman as More had done, the Queen's good
servant but God's first. It was the "magic press" of Robert Persons
which memorialized Campion's triumph when it turned out the
martyr's *Ten Reasons,* a substantial contribution to the tradition
which we have been tracing from the time of Thomas More. Persecution drove Persons to France. At Paris he sat in a restless state
with the very leader of the Catholic resistance, William, later
Cardinal, Allen. In May of 1582, a Jesuit, one William Crichton,
arrived from Scotland and brought Persons and Allen with him
to his conferences with the Duke of Guise. He had with him a
plan devised and pledged by Esme Stuart, Duke of Lennox, a
hope for deliverance from the oppression of Elizabeth. Persons
hesitated to play a part which made him emissary to Philip to
seek his support. Philip refused and the affair lingered on until
Lennox met his downfall.

For this episode Persons has been harshly judged by many an
historian. In their interpretations they have devised a "temporal"
category for the Catholic dissenters, like Persons, as opposed to
the "spirituals" who were above the chicanery they have found in
this most jesuitical of Jesuits. A more gentle judgment has been

this: "Looking back we now recognize how great Father Persons' error was; but it is also easy to see that with the approbation of the pope and of Allen and the other leading English Catholics living abroad, he had many excuses. He certainly did not contemplate the subjection of his country, but its liberation from an insufferable burden."[2]

Seen as a whole Persons shows himself something other than a specialist in political intrigue. To the constructive work of the English College at Rome he added, after the Lennox affair, several other institutions to educate Englishmen, the last being St. Omer, which was one day to educate the Carrolls and other American Catholics. His *Spiritual Directory* provided a *vade mecum* for his missionaries in their struggles for self-conquest. He labored on with controversial publications. Most remarkable was the *Conference on the Next Succession,* a pseudonymous book, which was attributed to him and which he never disavowed. In it the author makes a devastating attack on the divine right of kings theory and with impressive erudition explodes the validity of its honored law of hereditary succession by which monarchs were infallibly to come by their crowns as the anointed of heaven. What Thomas More devised in the fantasy of *Utopia,* Persons thrusts into the arena of practical politics of the moment in England; he demands that the succession of kings be settled directly by the people. This was in 1594.

The crossing of political and theological currents of thought had been the pattern of Persons' mature life as it had been More's; and spiritual distress had brought him to this critical analysis of the origin of civil authority. He did not reason to the same depths as Bellarmine, but he saw that the law of royal succession had played a villain's part in the tragedy of the English Catholic. "But to make subject to no Law or limitation at all," he brooded, "and to free them [kings] from all obligation unto the whole Bodie where they are the Heads, as though they had been bred Kings from the beginning of the world, or as though the Common-

wealth had been made for them and not they for the Commonwealth, were to bring all to such absolute tyrannie as no Realm
ever did or could suffer among civil People."[3]

In an effort to avert the return of a Stuart seventy years later, a
Jesuit baiter honored Persons' foresight in republishing his *Conference* with a necessary disclaimer, however, of any jesuitical
influence. To one who would observe the growth of Anglo-Amer-
ican democracy this outgrowth in Persons' thought under the
press of evolving events is indeed revealing of non-Spanish influ-
ences deriving from More's tradition.

Persons was badly badgered for the liberal aspects of his pleas.
At times he seemed bewildered and even confused in reconciling
church-state relationships. Perhaps this was to some extent due to
the Paris interview and embassy to Philip. He had lost the freedom which a controversialist must have in advancing liberal
views. His enemies in England quickly attacked his weakness.
Persons complained of the penal laws; but, responded his opponents, had not the Christian ruler the obligation to suppress heresy
with such laws? Persons had not only the record of medieval history to explain but the ever-zealous secular arm of suppression
wielded by his patron Philip II. In spite of these difficulties, Persons did take decisive stands in the tradition of More. There is the
instance in *Certain Reasons,* for example, when Persons made the
supposition that the Protestant religion be true and then considered if he would as a convinced Catholic be obliged to enter this
religion, which he did not believe to be true. "Yet should I be
condemned for going amongst them," he concludes, "for that in
my sight, judgment and conscience (by which only I must be
judged), they must needes seemes enemyes to God. . . ." Faced
with this remark, Professor W. K. Jordan, a sharp critic of Persons, correctly observes: "Unless Persons was completely insin-
cere, he came close to enunciating a doctrine of general toleration.
. . . If we interpret him correctly, he came close to asserting that

a man is judged, not by the truth of his beliefs, but by the devotion and sincerity with which he adheres to those beliefs."[4]

We need not claim too much for Persons, however, particularly since we are confronted with an inadequacy of biographical scholarship. The turn of events brought a principle of toleration to his mind and he communicated it to others even if he did not resolve the problems it created in the face of contemporary and past institutions. He tells us that men were looking in the direction of political democracy as a means of clearing the roadblocks to religious liberty. Much of what Persons wrote was unacceptable to many of his confreres in "priest holes" and secluded Catholic residences in England, but they would hardly ignore this contact with More's principle of toleration and Persons' reach forward toward a democratic principle of succession. At these points he supported the church-state tradition we have been tracing. Where he was at odds with this trend, he brought about clarifications by the vigorous discussion his writings provoked.

Catholics in England did not need Persons to urge them to remove the ruler who was persecuting them. They, too, had a heritage of self-government, at least in Parliament, and the desire to enlarge it at the cost of the crown sprang naturally into the minds of many. These were the sixteenth-century wellsprings of English political history which in the next century finally closed with Parliament supreme over the crown. For the moment, however, the Catholics' problem in following this inspiration was to reconcile it with the injunction of the New Testament and Christian tradition to reverence and obey the civil ruler. Would it be legitimate totally to reject the rule of Elizabeth for another? The question was put to Pope Pius V, who in turn gave an answer, but only after much delay and in a manner far removed from the fanfare of a proclamation.

When the pope's bull, *Regnans in Excelsis,* was issued, fresh coals were heaped on the fire being built under obstinate Catholics.

Some English Catholics were on Spain's side; now Pius V had
joined them. Furthermore, he commanded the remaining loyal
Catholics to withdraw allegiance to the queen and in this way
they became allies of the alien devil, Philip. In yielding to this
order, English Catholics were committing themselves to the belief
that the pope had the power directly to depose a civil ruler. Even
among the most ardent advocates of Spanish assistance in changing the rule, English Catholics did not believe that all of these
things followed or that any of them were found in *Regnans in
Excelsis;* nevertheless, panic struck their ranks like a lightning
bolt.

In this crisis, Cardinal Allen, for some time leader of the
Catholic resistance and the same interlocutor with Persons and
the Duke of Guise in the dramatic Paris meeting, demonstrated
the needed sagacity in his policy as well as in his work, *Defense of
English Catholics.* Against such an onslaught as the papal bull
brought, he had to seize the central issue, not merely to win an
argument, but to save the English Catholic and his embryo
tradition. Thomas More had believed that he could be both God's
servant and the king's without any conflict of loyalty. He sup-
posed, however, that the king did not tamper with his conscience
and beliefs, which were committed by God to a spiritual authority
distinct from the king and the state. This tradition now had to
deal with the reverse side of the coin that read, "render to Cæsar
the things that are Cæsar's," and to consider what things were
God's; to define the nature of the church and declare its limitations.

Actually, to win an argument with those who questioned the
loyalty of the Catholic in England in assenting to the bull, Allen
had only to show that nowhere in the bull did Pius V command
Catholics to withhold civil obedience. The action of excommunication was less of a problem, since it was personal and
private in its force, excluding Elizabeth from the sacramental life
of the church. In the final analysis, the document added up to a

description of Elizabeth as an unjust ruler, which few Catholics would deny. As such they were free, even by the natural law, to change this condition which amounted to tyranny. But even in evaluating the practical political condition of Elizabeth and her rule, the pope gave evidence that he was rendering merely a private opinion that one *could* possibly justify an extreme measure. There is indication that he was leaving this final judgment up to Englishmen. Thus it is as Professor J. W. Allen has said: "The notion that a Catholic always in his heart believed that the pope had power to depose a king, was a delusion deliberately fostered by controversialists, who should have known better."[5] The remarkable implication of *Regnans in Excelsis* was that it was implicitly appealing to a democratic principle of self-determination as a means of restoring religious liberty. The implication of Pius V was close to Thomas More's description in *Utopia* where the people's power to remove a king was just such a safety valve.

This interpretation does not strikingly emerge from the text of *Regnans in Excelsis*. That is why passages from it were used to impugn the patriotism of English Catholics. There is no doubt that Pius V, who was removed from the sources of knowledge about peculiarly English traditions and actual conditions, wrote against a background of a medieval papacy which exercised the power of deposition by the practical influence of its prestige. "This medieval formula," explains Sturzo concerning the deposition of Elizabeth, "which held good when a vassal was bound to his sovereign by a kind of free proffer, a contract *sui generis* which formed the feudal bond of sovereignty, had not the same sense in the period of the formation of the modern state, which was growing up around the idea of the nation." Pius declared, for example, that, "She [Elizabeth] has forfeited her pretended title to the aforesaid kingdom. . . ." but the weaker phrase follows which says Catholics are *"released* from that oath."[6] He had previously mentioned in detail how the oath involved accepting laws that followed upon Elizabeth's control of religious belief as head of the Church of England. Where he later commands that no one obey her mandates and laws, the whole context indicates that the reference is not to all laws but only to those which are illegitimate in that they are usurpations of spiritual authority.

Fortunately, Allen steered a wiser course here than in his direct political efforts. The diversionary arguments of his opponents did not, as often happened with Persons, lead him far astray from the all-important issue. On a practical level, he forbade discussion in the seminaries of the theoretical question of deposition. He was able to say: "Not any one priest of the Society or seminaries can be proved by the adversary to have absolved in secret confession any one man living from his allegiance; or to have ever either in public or private dissuaded any one person in the realm from his obedience in civil causes to the queen." To the charge that Catholics kept ecclesiastics entirely from under the authority of the queen he explained: "There is a great difference to say she is not to rule the bishops in causes ecclesiastical, or in matter of ministering the sacraments, preaching and doctrine; and to say she is not queen or governor over the clergy, or that priests or ecclesiastical persons be not her subject." He then concluded by emphasizing his main principle, which Elizabeth tried to claim that Catholics did not hold: "They [ecclesiastics] are bound . . . to order and obedience of their kings; and to observe their temporal and civil laws made for peace, tranquility, and temporal government of their people. . . ."[7] The present difficulties could be resolved on this principle and Allen knew that Elizabeth could not concede the point and make good her case; for Elizabeth was attempting "to rule bishops in causes ecclesiastical . . . and doctrine. . . ."

In the practical situation of *Regnans in Excelsis,* Allen did not hesitate to interpret in favor of civil authority, even though he strongly favored an end of Elizabeth's reign and was actively working toward the succession of another to the throne. More extreme statements were made by others, such as the following:

"If the Pope's Holiness should charge us to obey in this sense, to advance an enemy to the English crown, we should never yield to it: as by no law of nature or nations, or of man to be compelled thereunto; no more than to commit adultery, incest, or to murder ourselves, our children, our parents."[8] Such a papal action would be in the role of an Italian temporal prince, the very role which More warned Henry not to aid, and not that of a supreme spiritual pastor. Pius V seemed to sense all of these possible implications in giving a view of the English Catholic's problem of conscience. And when English Catholics remained loyal to Elizabeth in the conflict with Spain they deepened the impression in their political tradition of a Gelasian reserve which they demanded of the papacy in the temporal issues in their own land.

In these differences between Allen's so-called "Spanish party" and those who chose to continue the *status quo* in England, we must not obscure the position of Allen. Support of a change in succession did not imply acceptance of papal power directly to control the civil authority and depose a temporal ruler. Change of rule could proceed on the justifying argument of tyranny, an appeal to the innovation of popular approval of rulers.

Out of these conflicts Allen and other Catholics developed important details of that political tradition which stretched back through More to the Gelasian formula. We even find the basic formula of Gelasius in Allen's writings and a discussion of the problem which conditions of his own day posed in the face of it. "The power political hath her princes . . . and the spiritual her prelates," he explained with the formula of Gelasius. He then complicated the picture of the two distinct powers when he suggests how the Christian Commonwealth differs from the pagan. "These powers, when the princes are pagans, [are] wholly separate; but in the Christian commonwealths joined, though not confounded." When are the temporal and spiritual confounded? "Nor yet the spiritual turned into the temporal," Allen answers in an accusation of Elizabeth and Henry, "or subject by perverse

order, as it is now in England, to the same. . . ."⁹ One then feels
that Allen may have been taking a position at the other extreme
of such a "perverse order": "The civil, which indeed is the inferior,
[is] subordinate, and in some cases subject to the ecclesiastical.
. . ." The inferiority and subordination of which he spoke was
one of natures; the end of the church was something in quality
superior to that of the state. The very nature of man, church, and
state accounted for this conclusion.

This nature of things would not seem a basis for his conclusion
that the temporal was subject to the spiritual authority, for subjection implies an interference in the natural order of things. Yet
Allen accepted this natural order of things, which establishes
autonomy in church and state. But what were these "some cases"
which disturbed this order? "So long as the temporal state," he
explained, "is no hindrance to the eternal felicity and the glory of
Christ's kingdom, the other intermeddleth not with her actions,
but alloweth, defendeth, honoureth, and in particular commonwealths obeyeth the same," then there is no occasion for subjection
of state to church. Clearly, a case of tyrannical violation of freedom
of conscience would justify, according to Allen, direct action by
the church. The church somehow must have a means to save such
souls in distress, and Allen would not seem to stop short of a
means which, strictly speaking, were natural only to the temporal
order. In speaking of what the state must do positively for the
church, Allen was inexact. Obedience to the church by the state
was not in the essence of the relationship, as phrased; allow-
ance of the church is. *Defendeth* and *honoureth* are sufficiently
broad to remove them from implying subjection to the church,
though not entirely. The same cannot be said of *obeyeth*.

Allen was taking account of medieval practices as well as the
conditions of the moment which challenged solution. The task
seemed insuperable, and perhaps he used the wrong approach.
Fundamentally, however, the church, according to Scripture and
the Christian tradition, was a mystery for Allen. There was the

added complexity of human institutions and the state in England during a period of historical transition. In spite of it all, Allen did elaborate the Catholic political tradition of the autonomy of the state which was basic to the Catholic's patriotic loyalty during the events at the turn of the century. Catholics were faithful during Elizabeth's contest with Spain. Yet the charge of treason was intimated anew during the reign of James I and largely centered around his celebrated Oath of Allegiance. Church-state concepts would further develop during his reign, which will bring us to the immediate circumstances of the Maryland emigration.

CARDINAL BELLARMINE AND JAMES I

James I was the son of Mary, Queen of Scots. It was through her, the grand-daughter of Henry VII, that he became heir to the throne of England as well as Scotland. In 1603 he succeeded to the throne of England, vacated by Elizabeth's death; he brought with him a church-state experience quite different from what she had. The Scottish kirk was not pliant in royal hands, and the Calvinistic spirit, so deeply rooted there, went before James into England, there to vex him throughout his reign in the form of Puritanism. Calvin's position was at the other extreme of Elizabeth's, the state inclining toward subordination to the church. It was in reaction to the Presbyterian ecclesiastics in Scotland and this inclination that James fostered his conviction of the divine right by which kings held their power. In this situation it was further to his advantage to speak of separation of church and state; and, finally, to see in the law of royal succession, by which he came to two thrones, an expression of divine wisdom and sanction.

This was hardly the climate to instill that salutary restraint which Gelasius thought proper for secular and ecclesiastical rulers in their relations with each other. In England, James found not only the tradition of penal laws against Catholics, but a rapid growth of Puritan animosity against Catholics and their influence.

Above all, he had to respect the spirit of nationalism, which reached its high-water mark during the reign of Elizabeth; and this meant continued pressure toward religious conformity to the religion of the state. James had to work at bolstering his royal power and the theory that supported it. However much James wanted to play the philosopher, he had to deal with these matters in pragmatic terms.

Catholics soon felt the heel of the high-striding monarch when Guy Fawkes was arrested in the vaults beneath Parliament the day before it was to convene in 1604. The usual rumors of popish plots had been more persistent than usual, and the device of an anonymous note was contrived which disclosed a scheme, known as the Gunpowder Plot, to blow up Parliament. The reign of Elizabeth and the Catholic connections with Spain paved the way for the public reaction that followed.

James' response came the same year when he redoubled the penal laws against papists. The following year he formulated an Oath of Allegiance, intended for Catholics and ostensibly designed to make them promise loyalty to the king and abjure any foreign power. "I do truly and sincerely acknowledge in my conscience before God," the Catholic had to say, "that our sovereign Lord, King James is lawful and rightful king of this realm."[10] In swearing this, one need not have implied that he accepted James' theory of royal succession or rejected the point Persons had made that the power of determining succession was in the people. However, the same was not true of the next part: "That the pope, neither of himself nor by any authority of the church or See of Rome, or by any other means with any other hath any power or authority to depose the king or discharge any of his subjects of their allegiance and obedience to his Majesty." What is implied here had been a matter of theoretical controversy both as to the subtlest elements of the temporal and spiritual societies as well as to the past acts of medieval pontiffs.

Understandably, many would not be able to advance to this

second step. "What it does do," McIlwain so well observes, "is to deny emphatically that the pope can ever override this division by exercising the secular power of deposition under pretext of a spiritual end. Had the act done this and nothing more than this, in straight-forward and unequivocal terms it seems probable that it would have been enough to drive a wedge between those Catholics who held and those who rejected Bellarmine's doctrine of a papal power indirect to interfere in a secular matter *ad finem spiritualem* [for a spiritual end], and it would have been extremely difficult to dispute James' frequent assertions that his oath was 'merely Civil.' "[11]

There were those who disagreed with Bellarmine and inclined toward Gallicanism. They believed that papal authority was greatly circumscribed by the bishops within a country, who historically had looked to the king to maintain the demarcation. Royalists, too, among the Catholics would tend to support the king in his contention if stated without ambiguity. Such ambiguity unquestionably stands out later in the Oath; but it seems to the present writer that in this second step James was demanding acceptance of his position as head of the Church of England, for he presumed to define what the nature of the church is. He seemed to be demanding that Catholics accept his divine right theory, for he anathematized the growing democratic belief that popular appeal against a king is lawful in the event that he is grossly unjust and tyrannical. He seems to deny the Catholic the right in such an appeal to consult the church's supreme authority on the morality of the political conduct involved, aside from the practical decision which may be left to the Catholic's judgment. Thus, even at this point in the Oath many a loyal subject could take pause.

A third part of the Oath none but the confused and pusillanimous would accept: "I do further swear that I do from my heart abhor, detest, and abjure as impious and heretical, this damnable doctrine and position, that princes which be excommunicated or deprived by the pope may be deposed or murdered by their subjects or any other whatsoever. . . ."[12] James here appealed, not to the Gallican Catholic, but to the anti-papal forces outside the Catholic circle. In doing so he overplayed his hand. His second step could have driven a wedge in the Catholic party, but the implications of James passing judgment upon a doctrine in such terms as "impious and heretical" provided the rallying point of Catholic opposition that reached back to the time of More, an opposition which had never been relinquished or gainsaid. James stood under More's indictment of Henry for assuming power over religious belief. The church was with James as it had been with Elizabeth—the subordinate entity that Cardinal William Allen had criticized as "a perverse order." "Could it be said of this requirement," McIlwain correctly observes, "that it had nothing to do with things spiritual? The king here demands that English Catholics shall deny the pope's authority in secular matters, but what is he himself doing when he sets himself up to adjudge as heretical a doctrine believed by the majority of Catholics? Could James expect the pope to regard the line of division between the secular and the spiritual when he so ignores it himself?"[13] Evidently James is not playing the disinterested philosopher. When he adds "murdered" to "deposed" he is close to the demagogue, using *regicide* to insinuate accusations.

There were many ropes to the Oath, and some Catholics reached a frantic hand at one they thought they could grasp; but inevitably it would lead to ensnarement. Those who saw the implications and did not reach, were still victims, if in a different sense. They had refused an Oath of Allegiance to their king, they had demurred before the symbol of their loyalty to England. This was the way the recusant appeared to the undiscerning glance of his fellow Englishman. Any Catholic effort to win an acceptable oath was so much fumbling because the whole business of James' Oath making was begun in bad spirit. But most important of all to James was the fact that the Oath was a decisive blow against those who fought his absolutism in theory and practice. In a sense, certain Protestant elements were ensnared by the Oath controversy, particularly the Puritans; the anti-papal lure put them on the side of the king and the case he was making for the fullness of power, thereby putting them in a position of weakness when they later challenged that expanded power.

It was on these very grounds of divine right and absolutism that Cardinal Bellarmine strode with the sureness that he had as the leading apologist among the Catholics. James' modesty as philosopher did not prevent him from personally taking pen in hand against his adversary. In the exchange of tracts Bellarmine reflects the tradition which we have been tracing, but he deals more directly with the most complicated elements of church-state relations. He does this even when he states the *duo sunt* formula of Gelasius: "Though now in Christian lands the *Respublica Christiana* and the *Respublica Politica* are united and, as it were, interfused, since the subjects of each are the same, yet are they properly and truly two kingdoms, distinct in origin, aims, laws, external forms, and magistracy." Surely this was the situation of the English Catholic as he faced the Oath from one side and on the other the admonitions of the theologian. Catholics often did not know if a given action in the concrete was essentially temporal or spiritual. The nature of each authority, however, taken apart from the individual citizen, was more capable of clear analysis, and Bellarmine, like Cardinal Allen, put down principles in this category. It was significant, however, that Bellarmine gave another elaboration to the Gelasian notion, somewhat along the lines Persons had suggested. After explaining that one society is concerned with particular spiritual functions and the other with temporal, he alludes to their origins: "The Christian republic was instituted by Christ . . . the civil state, on the other hand, took its origin from human agreement." If we take this explanation together with Bellarmine's previous consideration of the position of the individual under the two authorities, we see that the consequences for the king are quite distressing. The temporal order is "somehow" subordinated to the spiritual and its head. Within the temporal order itself, the king is subordinate to the people whence civil authority derives, according to Bellarmine. "The king," Sturzo remarks, "thus found himself in a vise, between the pope above the people below."[14]

How then did the pope exercise this authority over the king and still respect the Gelasian *duo sunt* formula? Bellarmine sees that the pope may not depose a king as he would a bishop, for such an action would be direct and as such reserved to the temporal order. It must be indirect, and with Bellarmine this seems to mean that the measure is essential to the spiritual welfare of souls entrusted to the pontiff. But surely the deposition of a temporal prince is a directly secular action, whatever the end in view. Bellarmine does not seem consistent, but the general burden of his contention is unmistakable in the context of the persecution of English Catholics. The pontiff *somehow* has the power to deal with these temporal conditions which are bringing disaster to souls. He was led to defend deposition because his approach to the church-state problem had been dominantly from the medieval background which provided an entirely different context than that of seventeenth-century England. Whether the spiritual authority may in an emergency use direct temporal means at a moment of breakdown in society in the interest of justice is indeed a profound and difficult question. The *somehow* was not clarified. Perhaps the best the English Catholic could say was that if the state and its head had respected the limits of its authority and the rights of its citizens, adjustments with the church would have *somehow* been made. The first step was for James to take, and the Oath was clearly in the wrong direction.

The Englishmen of the seventeenth century could take a long range view, though without solving this immediate problem. A democratic movement had by this time gathered momentum and promised to remedy the basic sources of disorder. Bellarmine had stated some of its premises against James' divine right theory. Perhaps he should have made the application of the moderate Gallicans who said that deposition was in the hands of the people. Had this been an accepted principle in Henry's reign the plight of Catholics would not have developed, but by the reign of James its application would not have been made in favor of Catholics anyway. It would only be through a period of institutional growth that toleration and religious liberty would be matured and made secure by written constitution. The alternative for Catholics was to suffer for their faith, and the church would painfully have to record the loss of the weak. It is understandable that Bellarmine was pressed to a means that was doubtfully spiritual in order to repair the breakdown in political life which was driving English Catholics to their tragic alternative.

This tendency toward democracy in the spiritually beleaguered extended to the New World. The Marylanders could, in a sense, turn back the clock to days before the Act of Supremacy and the penal laws. They could start anew with the peace of toleration which a new political life could include. But even the Marylanders, as they pursued their ideals, had their stormy years as events in England touched their shores from time to time. They too had to live a faith whose church was a mystery and gospel a sacrifice. As things stood with James and Bellarmine, they had not resolved this mystery that enveloped the middle ground between church and state. James was unrealistic in pretending that the distinction between the two eliminated such ground. Bellarmine, in using the term "indirect power," implied the idea of the state itself as a perfect society, and yet he faced up to the fact of mixed temporal and spiritual matters. His more general principle, that the spiritual authority must *somehow* transcend this autonomous temporal order in mixed matters that affect her goal, could not have failed to win acceptance among Catholics, even though they may have rejected deposition or espoused varying degrees of Gallicanism. In the course of time the *somehow* came to take the shape of a demand for toleration from the state; not official establishment, nor dangerous assumption of spiritual functions by the state, but a temporal condition of freedom to pursue its spiritual function with spiritual means was the church's goal.

In spite of the reasoning of Bellarmine, all did not reject the Oath. Pope Paul V in direct terms warned English Catholics against it, and yet the highest ecclesiastical authority in England took it, the Archpriest Blackwell. Upon the death of Cardinal Allen in 1594, Blackwell functioned in England with certain delegated episcopal powers. In a spirit of compromise he hoped eventually to win concessions from James for taking the Oath. He explained that the pope was commanding what was wrong, misunderstanding the nature of the Oath, which meant that Blackwell was not bound. He may have accepted the pope's reasoning and principles without agreeing that they were relevant, a dangerous course in the light of the common practice of external obedience which one gives for the sake of discipline even when one may not internally assent to the pontiff's view.

Roger Widdrington, a Benedictine missionary in England, spoke out in more Gallican fashion in support of the Oath. He defended James's reasoning for some time and in 1634 reproduced several of his own tracts under the descriptive title, *A Patterne of Christian Loyaltie*. It was a plea in the vein of Watson, who took a similar position at the time of Pius V's excommunication of Elizabeth. Blackwell, Widdrington, and Watson made up what might be called the radical influence. Aside from their differences regarding the authority of the pope over the other bishops, they all emphasized the duties of patriotism. They were susceptible to the royalists' delineation of a conspiracy with foreign powers against England as promoted through English papists. The struggle with Spain during Elizabeth's reign found the majority of English Catholics with these radicals on the side of the excommunicated Elizabeth, and this continued during the reign of

James. Thus Catholics chose to work out a settlement within the existing framework of politics without any revolutionary proposals, even though the pope seemed to suggest a different course. This was true of those who sought a system of succession which depended on popular choice. In this way the experiences of Elizabeth's and James' reigns confirmed English Catholics in the belief that in practice temporal matters would not be directly affected by allegiance to Rome.

Because Blackwell stated in his book, *A Large Examination,* that the majority of English Catholics probably accepted the indirect theory of Bellarmine, we cannot say that they all held to what Bellarmine considered an application of this theory, the power to depose. Some doubtless held that merely in the temporal order the people have the right to depose a tyrant. It is not certain that a majority held that the pope may compel them to this action, and the evidence for this is the reluctance of English Catholics to consider this view when Pius V released them from their allegiance to Elizabeth. They were not certain that the course papal sources were suggesting would lead to liberation, but perhaps to protracted foreign occupation. This seemed to be their decision, and it was clearly in the temporal order. By his reserve in promulgating the Bull *Regnans in Excelsis* and in phrasing his message, Pius V indicated that this ultimate decision was in the temporal sphere.

In time Blackwell was unable to defend his position and relinquished his authority, delegated and limited, over the secular clergy. The effect of this on the regular clergy, the religious orders, was not as great as might be imagined, particularly in the case of the Jesuits who received directly from Rome their faculties of dispensing the sacraments. It was, however, a great handicap for the Catholics to live in England without the benefit of a resident bishop, but no other arrangement was tolerated by the government. England was in fact a mission, directly under the *Propaganda Fidei* at Rome. There was no diocesan structure in which a bishop could function should he come. As the whole ecclesiastical organization of the country labored under so many limitations, it was no surprise that harmony did not prevail and that many were fearful of entrusting another like Blackwell with added measures of authority. Beneath the surface of all this was a squabble between the religious orders and the secular clergy which exerted no small influence on the alignment of doctrines held on church-state matters.

Conditions drifted on for more than ten years after the Blackwell affair and the Oath controversy. In the early 1629's rumors spread of a restoration of an ecclesiastical authority in England. Some believed that this would involve a bishop with full powers who would, at the risk of penalties, establish the ecclesiastical machinery found in every Catholic country. It was finally learned that Dr. Richard Smith had been sent by the Holy See. This was the man whom Cardinal Allen had designated head of the College of Douai. Before coming to England he had been given the See of Chalcedon which in some way seemed to give him quasi-episcopal power which he might exercise in England.

Whatever the actual intent, the laity were the first to give tangible expression to the general concern for what might be the plans of Dr. Smith. More than three hundred English Catholics signed a Remonstrance of Grievances which was drawn up in 1628. "To set up any new tribunal," they bluntly warned, "with certain forms for the administration of justice, differing from or foreign to what is already established by law, or, still worse, contrary to the same, is the crime of high treason." The consequences to themselves were important: "The slightest complicity therein is a capital crime, entailing forfeiture of all property and perpetual imprisonment."[15] Why should the arrangements for the church in England be changed by Smith since there had been no change in the circumstances which dictated the present *modus vivendi?* What of his own status? Though he may have had episcopal powers, there was no diocese in England.

To what extent these suspicions were justified we do not know. The importance to the Catholic political tradition was the way these three hundred laymen explained their own position in challenging Smith. They professed orthodoxy and obedience to legitimate authority. They admitted that the church had the right to ecclesiastical tribunals, legislation for the sacrament of marriage, and other spiritual matters, even though these matters had a mixed temporal element. Were they not, then, obliged to speak openly for these rights, to be intolerant of any modifications in the traditional forms? "Controversies of this kind appeal to a mixed power," the Remonstrance explained, "being partly temporal over our property and fortunes; and, as such, this authority has by our laws and statutes been made the subject, in varying circumstances, of various ordinances, confirmations, and alterations, no less in the reigns of Catholic than of Protestant kings, as seemed expedient in the eyes of ecclesiastical and political powers here."

The signers cannot be made to say that spiritual rights were relative. They certainly seemed aware that the church was making the best of a situation which was bad in terms of violated rights. Nevertheless, an important element of solutions in the field of mixed matters was relative, as seemed "expedient in the eyes of ecclesiastical and political powers here." This was saying a great deal. English Catholics, on this basis, did not need to feel compelled to reproduce some order that may have been conceived as ideal in another country, for example, Spain. Such freedom could and did lead to dangerous compromises, as with Blackwell. But this same freedom could and did lead to a fresh growth in church-state relationships in Maryland. Such freedom in principle respected the organic structure of the church as perennial but adjustable to that of the state, which itself was subject to even greater modification.

In the Remonstrance of Grievances we see a considerable development of a tendency to limit ecclesiastical authority. It was complementary to the constant struggle to confine the scope of the state. Upon analysis we have seen that the progress of this thought was along the general lines of Gelasius' insight. In the interaction of religious and political forces we see also that a solution to the Englishman's religious problems was related to the democratic modifications of existing political institutions; discussion was on the scholar's level but there was practical action by an ever-growing minority of ordinary citizens. When this growth was transplanted to the New World, it would proceed much more rapidly in soil that had not been exhausted by the strain of centuries. All of these things were the outcome of the challenge to be "the king's good servants." For the Catholic it meant that somehow the state must be made better and kings too; for then the integrity and autonomy of the state in the temporal order could be more fully respected and worthy of loyalty. In this accomplishment the church would be blessed by an expanded spiritual activity.

III. WHAT MARYLAND WAS WITHIN

THE CALVERTS AND THE STUARTS

"THE first act of King Charles," a Florentine ambassador of the time wrote, "has been to confirm all the members of the father's privy council in their offices, and on Monday last they took the usual oaths with the exception of Lord Baltimore, Secretary of State, who remarked to his Majesty that, as every one knew him to be a Catholic, he could not now serve him in the same high office, without exciting jealousy in others, nor was he willing to take an oath so wounding his religious feelings. It is said that his Majesty replied 'that it was much better thus to state his opinions, rather than to retain an office by equivocation as some did.' "[1]

Obviously, George Calvert, First Lord Baltimore, did not come to the secretariate of state as a Catholic. He did, in fact, become a Catholic only the very year that Charles took the throne from his father, James, in 1625. Before his conversion to Catholicism in 1625, he steered a course of service to James through the years of struggle with Puritans, Parliament and Catholics. Only a few years out of Trinity College, Oxford, he witnessed the great controversy over the Oath and saw the application of penal legislation to recusants. Calvert had to stand with King James here as he did against the Puritans when the Hampton Courts Conference left them unsatisfied; Puritans were compelled to conform to a church which was resisting their efforts to rid it of papist traits. During these early days, George Calvert came into

the service of the king. He went to Ireland as the king's observer
and had to report how poorly the policy of religious conformity
was proceeding.[2]

We have no record of how Calvert felt about the events he
witnessed as a member of Parliament during these years. Surely
he could not escape a debate with himself over the nature of a
church and state which was at the bottom of the problems of
religious conformity. Neither could he fail to hear the murmur of
growing opinion that challenged his monarch's theory of political
supremacy. Parliament strove to limit the royal power, particularly
in the exacting of funds, by the Great Contract of 1610. James
fought back after this concession and the following year adjourned
Parliament. In the course of the conflict that followed for a decade,
Sir Edward Coke, the English constitutional hero, had to pay
with his office of chief justice for his opposition to James. The
symbolic climax of the struggle came in the Great Protestation of
1621, which insisted: "That the liberties, franchises, privileges,
and jurisdictions of Parliament are the ancient birthright and
inheritance of the subjects of England, and that the arduous and
urgent affairs concerning the king, state, and defense of the realm
. . . are proper subjects and matter of council and debate in
parliament."[3] In a self-righteous rage, James tore the page from
the journal of Parliament and Coke found himself in prison.

Whatever his misgivings, Calvert by this time stood solidly on
the side of royalty. His bias increased as he moved from one office
to another into closer ties with the Stuarts. James made him clerk
of the privy council and allowed him to honor James' *alter ego,*
the philosopher prince, by translating into Latin the King's writings against Arminianism, that rationalist influence in Protestantism which opposed James' religious policy. It was perhaps no
coincidence that George Calvert found himself a few years before
his conversion to Roman Catholicism defending a proposed
Spanish alliance through the marriage of Charles. This turn in
James' policy provoked a general outcry which reached the House

of Commons in a petition against popery. Charles eventually married the French Henrietta Maria in the hope that French assistance would promote Stuart dynastic ambitions and free the crown from too much dependence on Parliament for the funds to pursue Stuart policy.

In this turning toward the Catholic countries of Europe many Catholics in England saw hope for alleviation of their harassed consciences. Those Catholics who had fully conformed to the Oath of James or who had foregone the practice of their faith could hope for a milder policy from the Stuarts, should they decide to be more fully committed to Catholicism. It was no more than a hope that some kind of influence from France would bring this about. The complicated reaction to the Stuart alliance with France, however, sustained the persecution against Catholics, even if it was somewhat slackened. Still Catholics found reason here to incline toward the royalist party, even though their political theory and developing tradition disposed them to respect the parliamentarian's cause; and many returned to Catholicism, some being among the court circle. As secretary of state in the privy council, Calvert became involved with those who sought an adjustment of conscience.

George Calvert became a Catholic in these circumstances. We do not know much of his spiritual *Aeneid,* except that it suddenly left him an alien on political shores so familiar to him from his long career in the service of James. Charles encouraged Calvert to remain in his council, indulging the Catholic's scruples on the oaths—striking evidence of the close bond between the Calverts and Stuarts. Before Calvert's conversion, James had already raised him to peerage, granting him the Manor of Baltimore in Ireland. When Charles sought another way to honor this Stuart friendship in the face of Calvert's resignation from the council, he found it in the promise of a colony in the New World, which would alleviate both temporal and spiritual distress.

Calvert knew from firsthand experience how important the Stuarts regarded the colonization of North America. England from the days of Elizabeth had been struggling toward a commercial supremacy over her rivals, the greatest of which was Spain. In cooperation with the Dutch, England broke the Spanish monopoly of trade. The Stuarts set themselves to the next task which was to speed the planting of Englishmen in the New World and thereby build up a strong support for the adolescent capitalistic economy of England. In return for the deposit of human population in North America would come raw material for English manufacturing, which in turn would find an additional colonial market for the manufactured products of the mother country. It was in keeping with these rudiments of the mercantilist theory to have private capital launch the new colonies, but it was the role of the crown to stimulate, charter and, if necessary, modify their politico-economic structure. The king and investors at times even looked to colonization as a solution to the religious problems of dissenters in the mother country.

George Calvert was a young man in his twenties when the story of John Smith and the Jamestown settlement was told. The London Company, which financed the 120 Virginia colonists, had the right to appoint through its council the officers who were to rule and, by 1619, had established an assembly of representatives from the several plantations. James, fearful of this growing autonomy, radically changed the original charter and made Virginia a royal colony whose governor and council were appointed by the crown. The assembly endured, however, and acted as a force for more democratic government in America.

When George Calvert was first appointed to an office concerned with the policy of colonization, the remarkable migration that led to Plymouth Rock was in progress. A group of religious-minded persons who were dissatisfied with the disabilities James imposed on their dissent departed from England for Holland. These Separatists, however, were possessed of a love of nationality as well as a desire for religious freedom, and in 1617 this led them to venture a colony that was English but removed by an ocean from the oppression of the mother country. They negotiated a patent from the London Company and set sail in the *Mayflower*. These true Pilgrims landed at Cape Cod, which proved to be outside the jurisdiction of the London Company. In this New World situation these Englishmen characteristically, as in Jamestown, expressed their conviction of self-government in the *Mayflower* Compact, which was to govern their affairs.

George Calvert had personal ties with the originators of another colonizing attempt with the same ideals that inspired the Pilgrims. His oldest son, Cecil, had married the daughter of Thomas Arundel, a Catholic of renown who sought a solution to the religious problem of his fellow Catholics. Walsingham had once proposed a New World colony for Catholics to Elizabeth but nothing had ever materialized. Arundel took up the idea the year of the Gunpowder Plot. He himself had first been imprisoned by Elizabeth. Then he went into voluntary exile and entered the service of Austria in which he won fame against the Turks. Though Arundel returned a Count of the Holy Roman Empire, recognition by the crown was inconstant under both Stuarts. This man and others in the same situation were among the group that sent George Waymouth to explore for a place of settlement. The project never succeeded, even though Waymouth touched on the Maine coast; yet a determination that had advanced so far would not die in the first failure.[4]

A few years before Calvert became a Catholic he took an active hand in colonization and, it seems, was concerned with its religious advantages to Englishmen. His position on the Newfoundland Committee led to the acquisition of the southeast peninsula in 1620. He then began to negotiate for a charter that was quite different from both the company and royal colony type found in Virginia. What Calvert intended to establish was a palatinate or proprietary colony. As the feudal term suggests, authority was to be vested in a family which retained authority of appointment to important offices. Yet there was to be a local assembly to "advise and assent" to the laws that were drawn up. One advantage of the proprietary colony to the settler was that the laws that governed it might take exception to those that prevailed in the mother country. This served to attract many with civil disabilities, which was according to the design of the crown. The proprietor operated his colony as a capital investment, selling and leasing, and looking to a return from certain fixed taxes. In 1623 Calvert received such a charter and went with his settlers to his Newfoundland palatinate called Avalon.

Calvert may not have previously known what Waymouth found in Maine, but what he himself experienced the first winter at Avalon in Newfoundland proved disheartening. Pioneering was challenging but it needn't be in such an unfavorable climate; after all, a vast continent stretched invitingly for hundreds of miles south. Calvert was an investor and decided to look in this direction before heavily committing his capital and energy. His eyes began to focus on Virginia.

In the interval before his arrival in Virginia, George Calvert became a Catholic, and this was substantially to modify his view of colonization. From what little we know of the days at Avalon, it appears that he seemed to accept the idea of its being open to religious dissenters; some had complained of his toleration of a priest and popish services.[5] These matters were now no longer impersonal policy. Charles had made friendly criticism of Calvert for his wildcat colonial schemes, encouraging him to enhance his family fortune with sounder investments. The king realized there was now much more involved in Calvert's colonizing when he resigned his office of principal secretary of state because of his religious beliefs and failure to take the Oath. Calvert, however, was himself to learn that these same problems were not to be solved in Virginia.

Although he had served on the Mandeville Committee, which was concerned with Virginia colonization, Lord Baltimore seems not to have anticipated what awaited him. His attempt to buy a tract of land from the Virginia Company received a cold rebuff. The letter which the Virginia Council sent to the king's privy council poignantly tells the plight of Calvert as a Catholic colonizer:

According to the instructions from your Lordship and the usual course held in this place, we tendered the oaths of supremacy and allegiance to his Lordship[;] [Baltimore] and some of his followers, who making profession of the Romish Religion, utterly refused to take the same. . . . His Lordship then offered to take this oath, a copy wherof is included . . . but we could not imagine that so much latitude was left for us to decline from the prescribed form, so strictly exacted and so well justified and defended by the pen of our late sovereign, Lord King James of happy memory. . . . Among the many blessings and favors for which we are bound to bless God . . . there is none whereby it hath been made more happy than in the freedom of our Religion . . . and that no papists have been suffered to settle their abode amongst us. . . .[6]

Confronted by this situation, Baltimore must have redoubled his determination, not only to win an irreproachable claim to New World land, but to make it a haven for his coreligionists. Only a palatinate could bring this about. This would put the colony's authority safely in Calvert hands, independent in large measure even from the king, securely beyond the reach of oaths and penal laws, Parliament and the privy council. Calvert could hope for such a Utopia. Did not Charles respect him for candidly rejecting the Stuart rationale as expressed in the Oath? After these calculations George Calvert took steps which would lead to a truly autonomous palatinate established by a charter from Charles.

THE MARYLAND PALATINATE

In the late days of feudal England, there was a common saying, "What the King is without, the Bishop of Durham is within." Durham was an extensive palatinate in the north of England, stretching to the Tweed river. Its degree of autonomy was still singular in the reign of James. It was this principality which served as a model for the proprietary colonies, as Sir Humphrey Gilbert's charter and Avalon's show. Since the times of Henry VIII, however, various limitations had been put upon Durham, thereby narrowing the autonomy of colonial charters fashioned after it. George Calvert lived to see many of the favorable events which promised him a colonial charter of this kind, but he died only a short time before his dream was realized beyond his greatest hopes. Charles granted to Calvert's eldest son Cecil not only the privileges of Durham already given in other proprietary charters but all the rights which Durham "heretofore ever enjoyed."[7]

The privileges of Durham at the height of its autonomy before Henry's reign were ideal for Maryland. The Normans had transported the concept of the old "marches" of Charlemagne to the feudal entities along the English northern frontier. Good government demanded autonomy for a place so far removed from the king's weal, a condition found in the New World colonies. The added autonomy granted to the Calverts was prompted by the King's friendship but perhaps more by Baltimore's distinctive purpose. As Charles M. Andrews explains: "He was under the impelling influence of motives and obligations that were more imperative than those of a mere colonizer—among which was the sacred duty of finding a refuge for his Roman Catholic brethren, an obligation which had been felt by the Arundel group for many years."[8] Great freedom was necessary to execute such a design.

"By reason of his royal jurisdiction," says one commentator of the head of the Durham palatinate, "he has all the high courts and officers of justice which the king has; and by reason of his royal seigneury he has all the royal services and royal escheates which the king has." The beleaguered Coke wrote, perhaps wistfully, of a palatine head: "The owner thereof, be he duke or earl, hath in that country *jura regalia* [kingly rights], as fully as the king had in his palace."[9] Charles in one particular passage puts down in summary "what Calvert was within" his palatinate:

The Proprietor has authority over matters criminal as well as civil, both personal and property and those of a mixed nature but in such a way that the above said laws be in accord with reason and be not repugnant nor contrary but, insofar as may be befitting, in accord with the statute laws, the customs and the rights of this Our English Kingdom.[10]

We see the spirit of English law reflected in this passage on the Maryland proprietor and throughout the whole charter. "Insofar as may be . . . in accord with . . . rights of this Our English Kingdom"—such phrases as these leave much room for interpretation and application. The meaning that was read into the consecrated formulas, particularly in references to English rights, expanded with succeeding generations. There was the case of the seventeenth-century appeal that Englishmen made to the medieval Magna Charta. Monarchs, on the other hand, tried to fix these rights by specific legislation. Elizabeth had tragically spelled out the traditional rights of Englishmen in reference to toleration when she established the penal laws. Such a tendency, to be explicit, discriminated against persons who were in the position of the Marylanders and Calvert. Undoubtedly their situation was an added reason why Charles allowed the charter to be broad and even vague in its provisions.

We see this advantage in Charter passages which bear on the religious status of the colonists. In one place which empowers the proprietor to interpret the Charter favorably to himself we find the express limitation, "Provided always that no interpretation is made by which God's true and holy Christian religion . . . would suffer any prejudice, diminution, or curtailment." In the light of the Oath controversy and Calvert's stand, this structure implies that Baltimore fixed the limits of civil authority in a way that he could not have found in the Stuart theory. This proviso demonstrated a respectful reserve toward the church and conscience that ruled out state absolutism.

But why is the term *Christian religion* used rather than Church of England? George Petrie says that the term refers to the Church of England, basing his reasoning on the practice in other documents. He concludes that a fixed relationship to the state was not prescribed; however, the colonists were free to establish the Anglican Church. Even the remote possibility of establishment of Anglicanism would have defeated the hopes of Calvert, which leads us to conclude that such was not the intention of the charter writers. At the other extreme another commentator says these words "at least technically include the possibility of the exclusion of all but Catholics, if Baltimore so willed."[11] This would be on the basis of extensive application of the rights of Durham. Such a meaning would be contrary to the commercial aspect of the Maryland project, which had to appeal to Protestants as well as Catholics if it would succeed. In addition to this interpretation from author and context considerations, the term *Christian religion* literally understood includes both Catholic and Protestant, particularly so in those days which were closer to the times of Christian unity.

The charter elsewhere assigns a more positive role to the proprietor, giving him the status of "patron of religion," as a Christian monarch or prince is styled. Europe had found such princes inclined to usurp spiritual authority. The same possibility suggests itself in Baltimore's case when we see the charter assign him the function of building chapels. How could they be anything but Anglican chapels? Did Catholics need his permission to build their own or could they even expect him to build them for Catholics? As the circumstances with Calvert, Charles, and the Maryland project clearly show, the charter was not intended to bring such involvements; and this meant that *Christian religion* was only a general reference, expressing a spirit rather than a prescription. Chapels could be authorized, or they need not be in order to be built, according to the vagueness of the passage. George Petrie correctly concludes: "It was not a time when things turned on technical interpretation of written documents. Historical forces were at work, and these . . . were . . . to determine the relation of church and state in Maryland."[12] The charter has its philosophy; but the sources of that philosophy—Calvert, Stuart, and English law, both recent and ancient—are diverse. The important point is that this heterogeneously-founded charter left the door open to further development of the tradition we have been tracing. This was precisely what the Virginia Council foresaw when they wrote to the privy council complaining of the charter phrasing. The king made no denial of the charge, thus giving further support for this interpretation of the charter.

Calvert was certainly a good royalist, and Charles treats him as such in the Maryland Charter. The king had put Maryland beyond parliament's reach, even if he could not put himself in a like position. He apparently set about fashioning the Maryland proprietor in his own image and likeness. Calvert was given great powers for granting immunities and other benefits. He was given full authority to assign and alienate land. There were many ways in which he could tax the inhabitants of his palatinate. Although reference was made to an assembly for Maryland, the proprietor felt secure in an ancient formula which weakly described its powers: "to advise and consent." "Absolute Lord," Charles agreed to call him. We wonder if the king fully realized what he was doing, whether he saw the potentialities of his creation. Calvert was a royalist, but he was not an absolutist, particularly in the church-state context of Stuart absolutism. Was Charles not, then, putting

Maryland beyond his own reach as well as parliament's, even though he might make the following vague restriction on Lord Baltimore: "[that he] always maintain faith and fealty and direct dominion to Ourselves"?[13] At minimum this charter agreement with Charles meant that Maryland was free to pursue a religious policy of its own making. The proprietor, on the other hand, found himself, by his fealty to the king, in a position that demanded constant administrative vigilance and deft diplomacy in order to gain the greatest advantages. This often meant that lesser gains had to be foregone in order to keep the good will of the royal government at home.

Cecil Calvert set about building his palatinate in the feudal style suggested by the charter. The several Catholic men of means who had been interested in Arundel's proposed solution to their problems would be attracted by the opportunity Maryland provided. These gentlemen would stake out estates which would grow into fine manors to honor their family traditions. Servants would be transported at their expense to work the fields, thus producing annual yields for the gentlemen investors. There were not to be any serf-noble relationships, however, even though the language of planning used feudal terms. Those who worked the land were known technically as indentured servants. After a stipulated period of time on the manor, five or ten years in the case of Maryland, their service would have repaid the cost of passage. They would then have the status of freemen. Freemen were in a position to acquire their own land holding, however small, and exploit the opportunity of the New World. Many others were able to come to Maryland as freemen, having sufficient means for passage and a modest beginning.

The gentlemen of Maryland held a position of great prestige. This would be true particularly during the first ten years of the colony. The number of freemen would grow only gradually as the period of indentured service was filled out. In time the gentlemen would find among their peers many who had risen, Horatio

Alger style, to economic and social standing. In the assembly the
gentlemen with their educational advantages would always be a
source of leadership for the freemen. The first few assemblies
would have them even numerically dominate many sessions. As
the fortunes of both gentlemen and freemen became commonly
affected by their relationship to the proprietor through his assess-
ments and direct controls, class demarcations declined. Because
the proprietor resided in England as over-lord, the Maryland gentlemen shared the lot of the other colonists. This community spirit
would find its natural expression in the assembly.

The charter freed Maryland from the laws of England and put
the colonists under the proprietor who had authority over matters
"criminal as well as civil, both personal and property and those of
a mixed nature." In this position, Baltimore operated like the head
of a company colony; in the latter case, however, the whole project and its personnel were entirely under the law of England.
When "property" or commercial matters became "personal" in
terms of human rights, the Marylander would have no detailed
law to protect him. There was only the general limitation that all
be "in accord with reason and be not repugnant nor contrary but
insofar as may be befitting in accord with the statute laws, the
customs and rights of this our English Kingdom."[14]

One might find in this general statement some basis for the
claim to all of the rights of Englishmen. But there is no more
than this, and for the Marylanders it would not be enough.
Maryland would be a sanctuary respectful and assuring of these
rights. It would be in the assembly that Marylanders would pro-
cure them in a written form, made sacred in law. In these terms
we see the potential of the charter passages providing for an assembly "to advise and consent." There was in addition the general
trend to expand parliamentary privilege in England, and the first
colonists seem fiercely to have imbibed the spirit of this movement; or perhaps it would be their days in the New World that
gave them their fierceness. One thus comes to reflect that in set-

ting Maryland beyond the reach of Parliament, and cutting the proprietor free from the king, the Marylanders found themselves close to self-government in the circumstances of their remote assembly.

CECIL CALVERT AND ANDREW WHITE

The Maryland Charter did not go quietly unnoticed by the general public in England. It had to be made public eventually, but the resourceful young proprietor saw to it that the seal of Charles was firmly fixed on the document before any debate began outside the palace. Virginians were the logical plaintiffs. They had objected to George Calvert's earlier projected settlement among them because of his religious affiliation. They now saw his scheme, so contrary to their own notions of religion and its place in the state, being planted across the Potomac in an area suited to their own expansion. On perhaps better ground, they contrasted the liberality of the Maryland Charter with their own, the royal replacement for the company charter. Governor Potts and his council had formulated their case against Calvert and the substance of it created a public attitude toward Maryland that Cecil Calvert had to mollify.

"There is intended to be granted liberties of a County Palatine," the Virginians had complained, "and there is no exception of writs of error, or of the last appeal to the King as by law ought to be." They put their finger on the passage which gave those "liberties . . . [which] any Bishop of Durham thus far ever held or could have held. This," Potts said, "is too general and uncertain," since it omitted the limits put on Durham in recent reigns. Anyone could see that these features made possible the evils the governor predicted would come about. Calvert "will people his [colony] with persons of all sorts whatsoever, different from other colonies in religious assertion." Such colonists "having power in themselves to manage their affairs free from all dependence on others," present a temptation alluring to Virginians, and this was in general a "very dangerous" condition.[15] Even though the king did not act on this kind of advice received by the privy council, it was up to Calvert to neutralize its influence on those who could in any way deter or help his colonial project. He had to take his case to the pamphlet press.

In addressing himself to the task, Cecil Calvert sought advisors, among whom was Father Andrew White who was to be the first missionary to Maryland. Like most educated Englishmen, especially clergymen, White drew his thought from both continental and English sources. His work, either as a student or a professor, had found him at various times in Spain, and at Liége and Louvain. If we are guided by the intimations of certain letters which he wrote to the Jesuit General at Rome while he was teaching, we may conclude that he was vehemently attached to the views of Thomas Aquinas and found fault with confreres who were not of a like mind. This circumstance with the evidence of his writings in the service of Calvert puts White in the philosophical tradition of Bellarmine and Suárez, a progressive formulation of a Christian basis for both democracy and toleration which is founded on the autonomous nature of church and state. His residence in England gave him a very live contact with the Catholic mentality that was taking shape under the force of English historical developments.

Calvert's case was put out with the help of this advisor in the pamphlet entitled *Objections Answered.* The author shows considerable boldness, for he does more than plead the case for the Catholic's patriotism; he attacks two accepted principles of church-state relations widely held in Protestant circles in England. The first is the alleged obligation of the state to suppress heresy. The author formulates the objection in the complaint that Maryland Catholics will be beyond the reach of penal laws which "were made in order to [bring] their conformity to the Protestant Religion, for the good of their souls. . . ." The reasoning here, according to some theologians of Calvinism, would have it a sin for one in authority to permit others to profess a false religious practice even if they are sincere. This is the *sin of permission,* as it is called. Compulsory external conformity to the true belief is better than none at all. To allow the people of Maryland to escape the pressure of this conformity "would scandalize common people here [in England]."[16]

The Maryland apologist found himself with the problem of Persons who had to reconcile the freedom of a misled conscience and the concern of the state for the condition of religion. It had to be admitted that the state could not be indifferent to religious conditions, yet the state could not directly interfere. Unfortunately for Persons, he became associated with Philip II's questionable reconciliation of the two principles. *Objections Answered,* however, was clearer and more unmistakable in its defense of conscience and in resistence to usurpations by the state. "Conversion in matter of religion," said *Objections Answered,* "if it be forced, should give little satisfaction to a wise state of the fidelity of such converts; for those who for worldly respect will break their faith with God doubtless will do it, upon a fit occasion, much sooner with men."

The author of *Objections Answered* here expresses the nucleus of his response to the attack of the Virginians. It is not a sin for the state to permit one to follow what his conscience sincerely believes to be true. It would be wrong to do otherwise, and it would also be imprudent for the state. The citizen is obliged to follow what he knows and believes in his dealings with God, the very bent which led Thomas More to the block at the Tower. There is also a suggestion of More's view that the church and conscience are beyond temporal authority. Faith with God is clearly superior in quality to the faith man keeps with the state, as Allen had stated. It was also well to state these principles in conjunction with pragmatic advantages they possessed. As the author says, "For voluntary conversions such laws [coercing conscience] could be of no use"; in fact they condition men to become faithless in their obligations to their country. A man who is sincere in his beliefs, on the other hand, whatever they be, will be a better citizen in this relationship of qualitative subordination of state to church.

The "faith with God" passage substantially deals with the second objection which assumes that a national state is inextricably bound up with its official religion. Conditions following upon the rise of the national state and the diversification of religious sects fostered this notion as did nationalism by the wars and rivalries it provoked. *Objections Answered* reflects this atmosphere in discussing a second criticism of the Maryland project: "The said Roman Catholics will bring in the Spaniards or some other foreign enemy to suppress the Protestants in those parts; or perhaps grow strong enough to do it of themselves; or that in time they may and will shake off any dependence on the Crown of England." It seems inconceivable to the objector that the Catholics were sincere in their respect for one's "faith with God." It also seemed impossible that one leave Protestantism without leaving the political dominion of England. A Catholic domination in Maryland or an alliance with a Catholic power were the only alternatives to be expected. Such was the only framework of discussion for the Virginians and those who took up their criticism. They had been reared in these suspicions, which Henry VIII created nearly a hundred years before when he obliterated the distinctness and autonomy of the church and its life in the state.

The pamphlet author could have adequately answered this objection by advertence to the fact of Catholic loyalty the past hundred years. Englishmen had heard this defense from Catholic apologists and knew it well. *Objections,* however, resorted to another polemic with greater freshness. It showed how absurd the objection was in the light of conditions in the New World. From our viewpoint we can see that such reasoning would not be conclusive because of the objector's radically different concept of church-state relations. That is why the most significant part of

Objections Answered was what we have quoted above: conscience was sacred and inviolable in God's sight, and it was in a distinct and superior order above the state.

This principle, enunciated in *Objections Answered,* is indeed distinguished as a part of the growth of a Catholic tradition. It puts the church in a secure position beyond the state without giving the state any of the dangerous prerogatives of "defending" and "reforming" which we find in Spain and England to be violating freedom of conscience. Insistence on freedom of conscience as a civil liberty and a civic virtue seemed the key to locating the church in a position favorable for growth. The happy formulation of the nature and consequences of "faith with God" was the result of something more than genius. It was the experience of suffering in human events and the blessing of an uncomplicated society in the New World which brought such enlightenment to these honest men.

Cecil Calvert began putting all of this theory into practice. He had to stay in England as lord proprietor and control situations which concerned the destiny of his colony. It would be through his brother, Leonard Calvert, Governor of Maryland, that he would carry out his policies. Cecil Calvert first concerned himself with the problem which a pluralistic society in Maryland created. This situation of Protestants and Catholics living at close quarters could lead to conditions which would disprove the case he had made in *Objections Answered.* Before the *Ark* and the *Dove* set sail, he formulated a policy to guide the governor and his commissioners in this matter.

"His Lordship required his said governor and commissioners," Baltimore's instruction read, "that in their voyage to Maryland they be very careful to preserve unity and peace among all the passengers. . . ." This was their obligation as English magistrates. Because civil authority in Maryland was at this time entirely in the hands of Catholics, a minority in England, Baltimore saw a dangerous situation in their exercising it over Protestants. And so he warned that "they cause all acts of the Roman Catholic Religion to be done as privately as may be. . . ." This initial reserve was extended to the discussion of religion among the colonists. English heresy laws forbade public preaching and discussion of alien doctrine as a threat to civil peace. Baltimore more simply told his officials, "Instruct all the Roman Catholics to be silent upon all occasions of discourse concerning matters of religion."[17] All of these directives were to be observed particularly on shipboard, but they were also to be norms of conduct in Maryland itself.

This return of Catholics to political authority stood in significant contrast to the reign of Mary Tudor. Baltimore showed a remarkable awareness of the delicacy of the religious situation. He saw the *fragilitas humana* that Gelasius insisted should be taken into account in granting authority, a consideration which prompted Baltimore to caution reserve in his governor. To the ordinary citizen he inculcated a lesson of charity, one peculiar to a Protestant-Catholic society. Fundamentally the admonition implied the reverent regard for conscience and one's "faith with God" to which More had been so sensitive. It was for Catholics in their position "to suffer no scandal nor offence to be given to any Protestants." Baltimore warned them that they were to prove his own claim to those who challenged his charter and its principle of religious freedom; nothing should be done "whereby any just complaint may hereafter be made by them [Protestants] in Virginia or in England." A good beginning on shipboard and in the first year in Maryland would assure that harmony so essential to preserving the peace in Maryland.

Baltimore clearly assumed the notion of religious toleration. He also implied the distinction of church from state, and in other directives to his officials he made this clearer. A few years after the above instruction, he prescribed the following oath for Maryland officials: "I will make no difference of persons in conferring offices, favors and rewards for or in respect of religion, but merely as they shall be found faithful and well deserving and imbued with moral virtues and abilities." And a later one had the official promise: "I will not by myself nor any person directly or indirectly molest or discountenance any person whatsoever . . . for or in respect of his or her religion . . ."[18] Such oaths reversed the conditions prevailing in England, not only to the advantage of Catholics but Protestants as well. This was no Stuart Oath, nor Test Act, nor the Calvinist's prescription of rule by the elect; and, at the same time, it was not what would be found in Spain. Though there were beginnings in France of the same spirit Baltimore showed, its advance was distinctively English—an outgrowth of a hundred years of development which converged in Baltimore's own remarkable circumstances.

Father White became lyrical in the atmosphere of sailing time and in his reflections on the auspicious policy that accompanied the enterprise. In his *Relation* he adverted to another part of Baltimore's instruction in which the good of religion was declared a primary objective:

The first and most important design of the Most Illustrious Baron, which also ought to be the aim of the rest, who go in the same ship, is, not to think so much of planting fruits . . . as of sowing the seeds of religion and piety. Surely a design worthy of Christians, worthy of Angels [*angeli*], worthy of Englishmen [*anglis*]. The English nation, renowned for so many ancient victories, never undertook anything more noble or glorious than this.[19]

IV. ACCORDING TO THE GREAT CHARTER

By November of 1633 Lord Baltimore had completed preparations for transporting the first Maryland settlers to America. The 360-ton *Ark* was fitted out at London, along with its 60-ton companion vessel, the *Dove,* and 128 passengers were ready to board for passage. For the most part these settlers seem to have been Protestants, since it is recorded that they took the Oath of Supremacy, which most Catholics would have refused. The oath-taking was carried out to forestall any charges that the Marylanders, upon their departure from England, had refused to perform this official act. The Catholics who were to make the voyage awaited the *Ark* and *Dove* in Cowes on the Isle of Wight, which was off the southern coast of England. In this way they could avoid taking the Oath without embarrassment to the proprietor. Protestants and Catholics thus united, the two crafts proceed southward toward the Canary Islands. The course was then west to the Barbados, where the skippers decided to delay in order to replenish supplies and make repairs. In doing this the *Ark* and *Dove* seem to have avoided Spanish galleons which would have attacked on sight. Although the *Ark* had twenty-four guns, Father White was not assured, feeling that they would have "become a prey of our enemies."[1]

On March 25, 1634, the Marylanders had made their way up the Potomac and stopped off temporarily on what was called St.

Clement's Island. There they were joined by the Protestant Captain Fleet from Virginia, who was familiar with the territory of Maryland and the Indians of the vicinity, and who could offer advice on where the first settlement could best be made. He guided the settlers a short distance farther down the Potomac to a bay that was then named St. Mary's. Here was the site of the first permanent settlement in Maryland, St. Mary's City. The Potomac was close enough to the Chesapeake Bay to have a salty tang and on a clear day the Marylanders could see the coast of the Virginia settlement across the broad river channel. To the east and north and several miles to the south lay the stretch of land which had lured the English gentlemen, the freemen and the indentured servants. This was on March 27, 1634—since known as "Maryland Day."

Among those who assisted at Father White's first Mass in America, Leonard Calvert was distinguishable. He bore the major burden of responsibility as governor. At his side were members of his council. John Lewger, its secretary, had not long been a Catholic but he had been known to the Calverts for some time. A man of greater prestige among the colonists, if of less influence with the Calverts, was the forthright commissioner on the council, Thomas Cornwallis. He evidently had standing as a military man, as the title *captain* given to him suggests.

The first year of the colony passed under the administration of this council. In military defense, leadership was with Cornwallis. John Lewger was responsible for the legal form of all land and tax transactions. He was under instructions from the proprietor and was supervised by the governor. Through his various commissions and instructions Lord Baltimore set down and clarified the function of these first officials who were joined together in the charter provision for a council. What prestige Leonard Calvert's name did not give him his position as president of the council did, for he received and enforced all of his brother's commissions.

After a year had passed, Maryland called its assembly into session for the first time, in March of 1635. It may be that Leonard Calvert, who in his capacity as governor became *ex officio* president of the assembly, called the first session. It is doubtful if he did so by some direction of the proprietor, but rather acted in accord with the general provision of the charter for a functioning assembly. From the political temperament which the Marylanders began to manifest during the first years of the settlement, we may conclude that he received considerable encouragement from the gentlemen and freemen. This was a first effort, and it was made by men who had had no experience in Parliament. The primitive surroundings did not give assurance to their first steps, but the assembly had the memory of a tradition of representative government, which ennobled the atmosphere of the narrow log structure that heard these first proceedings. No written record of the session has survived. Records of the following session tell us only that laws were passed and put into practice. The assemblymen revealed that they cherished the experience of self-government, for they provided by law that the assembly should convene every three years.

On the face of it, these do not seem startling achievements. As events would prove, however, the Marylanders had found themselves a new channel which would carry them along a historic course. They had given a liberal interpretation in favor of self-government to the vague charter provision that the assembly should "advise and assent." They had drawn up and initiated legislation according to their own mind and made it law, and thereby put Lord Baltimore in the position of one advising and assenting. They certainly had not acted according to the royalist mentality of Calvert, and it is doubtful if they were strictly applying the charter. Under the influence of the movement toward broadening parliamentary privilege, they had made strides more advanced than the Stuarts found in Parliament. When we consider that the colonists were not bound by the laws of the mother country, but were to fashion their own, their position was dynamic and revolutionary.

Leonard Calvert may not have been fully aware of the significance of these first official acts of the assemblymen. If they had thus drastically qualified the charter to their own advantage against the proprietor, they had also pared down the authority of the president when they provided that the assembly should by law convene every three years. In his violent rages, James had prorogued Parliament and thus prevented it from obstructing his own policies. His son Charles, playing the same absolutist role, also refused to convene Parliament. Subsequent events assure us that these historic moments were not forgotten when the assemblymen came to America. These were lessons they now shrewdly applied in their law for convening every three years. The assembly was now beyond the arbitrary reach of the governor. The Marylanders would make their own laws.

If the proprietor was dissatisfied with the shape his Maryland institutions were taking, he would have to wait some time before anything could be done about it. It might be months or even a year before news of its official actions reached England, and as long before he could give directions which he might hope would check these dangerous developments. In the meantime events in Maryland went on in what was the normal colonial fashion. There were such elementary occupations as building, plowing, and planting; trade was carried on. Father White and his companion, Father Copley, had established their quarters and chapel and had made excursions among the nearby Indians. The council began in the year 1636 to be concerned about Captain William Claiborne, the trader from Virginia who was pressing claims to land within Maryland territory both by his own activity around Kent Island and through his agents in London. Captain Cornwallis was promoting military readiness in this connection. He was aware of the use Claiborne might make of neighboring Indians, and

Cornwallis also heard from Father White of the Susquehannock Indians from the north, who were harassing the peaceful Indians of southern Maryland.

The internal peace of the pluralistic society of Catholics and Protestants, if we may judge by the *Court Proceedings* and other sources for the first three years, fulfilled the hopes which Cecil Calvert expressed in his instruction. In 1638, however, an incident took place which revealed what the Maryland religious design met in practice. Father White had left temporal matters to Father Copley, which meant that the land which was to support the missionaries was in his charge. Father Copley had chosen a zealous Catholic layman, William Lewis, to oversee the property and the work of the indentured servants connected with it. The house in which Lewis resided was near a path used by many passersby, among whom, as he noticed, were many Protestants. Apparently exceeding the discretion urged by Lord Baltimore's instruction, Lewis used his vantage point, according to complaints, to win over converts to Catholicism. When Lewis tried the same thing with some of his indentured servants, however, his behavior created a public issue.

The indentured servants did not have the services of a Protestant minister, which they found quite a hardship, but gave evidence of earnest practice of their religion. They had brought writings by English ministers to America with them in 1637 and assiduously studied them. Lewis, nevertheless, attempted to proselytize the devout Protestants. Offended by this, they began to speak of Lewis to their Protestant neighbors. As time went on a group was planning to join the servants in a petition to Virginia, in the hope that officials there would do something about Lewis. They were also asking for sympathy which might win them the services of some Protestant minister. The petition was already formulated and the signers about to gather when the council got word of the affair.

The members of the council saw immediately the danger of the impending action. They had the proprietor's instructions in mind, but they also saw the importance of these beginnings of possible intolerance in terms of the future of the whole colony and its distinctive institutions. They wanted no grounds for complaint in Virginia; they were determined to prove the case of *Objections Answered*. The Protestants were a minority in terms of influence, if not in numbers. Maryland Catholics could not forget that they too were once a minority; and, if they were realistic, had to look forward to the day when they might become the minority in Maryland. The council had powers to conduct a court and it immediately brought the plaintiffs and defendant before it.

Francis Gray, a servant on the Copley property, presented the petition to the court, but said that Robert Sedgrave, another servant, had drafted it. It contained the substance of the charges against Lewis. Lewis had said that their "ministers are ministers of the devil," and he "taketh occasion to call them [Protestants] into his chamber, and there labors with all vehemence, craft and subtlety to delude ignorant persons. Servants which are under his charge shall not keep or read what appertains to their religion,"[2] they complained. We do not know what Lewis answered to all of this, but the three Catholic magistrates were impressed with the case that was made against him. There was a general charge of disturbing the "public peace and quiet of the colony," which was specifically "against a public proclamation set forth to prohibit all such disputes"—a reference to the council orders drawn up in accordance with the instruction from the proprietor. The fine was five hundredweight of tobacco, to which Cornwallis added a similar fine.

One passage of the petition to Virginia read: "We beseech you . . . who have power, that you will do what lies in you to have these absurd abuses and heretical crimes to be reclaimed, and that God and his ministers may not be so heinously trodden down by such ignominious speeches."[3] Lewis claimed that the Protestant petitioners intended that the Virginia authorities "proceed against him as a traitor." In its decision, however, the court made public peace the only factor. Obviously, in the light of the distinctive principles of Maryland's colonial foundation, the magistrates could not bring a discussion of heresy into the case as the Virginians might, nor could they put an incident of religious controversy on a basis of treason, nor yet curb expression of religious opinion on all occasions. They had come to Maryland to escape such legal procedures. There is no doubt that the petition was inviting intervention by the Virginians and prosecution on the basis of non-Maryland law. Lewis tried to make this point, but to bring charges against the indentured servants for some kind of conspiracy involved more than judicial action within Maryland. Rather than provoke further criticism from Virginia the magistrates dismissed Lewis's charge as having "insufficient proof."

It seems that the whole settlement was satisfactory to Father Copley. Francis Gray had discussed the validity of his grievance with him, and, according to Gray's report, "Mr. Copley . . . blamed much Mr. William Lewis for his contumelious speeches and ill-governed zeal and said it was fit he should be punished."[4] As it turned out the court had refrained from entangling itself in spiritual matters and the clergyman from enlisting temporal authority for Lewis' proselytizing. Pope Gelasius would have been pleased with the delicacy and restraint of both authorities. The basis of judgment was in accord with the views of magistrate More; and Cardinal Allen could not have disputed the clergyman's view of the settlement.

The same year the Lewis case was tried, another arose involving conspiracy with the Virginians against the Maryland government. William Claiborne began to press his claim to Maryland territory with force, particularly in Kent Island. He succeeded in winning the Marylander Thomas Smith to his side as an open conflict of forces took place. Under the leadership of Thomas Cornwallis the Marylanders successfully defended Kent Island and captured the

traitor Smith. Smith was arraigned before the assembly instead
of the court because of the unsettled condition of Maryland law
and also because in English tradition Parliament had a quasi-
judicial function. The assemblymen soon came to believe that
capital punishment was the proper penalty for Smith.

Someone questioned the right of the colony to proceed with
capital punishment. Because they had no law of their own on the
matter, the assemblymen consulted the statute laws of England.
They felt that Smith's act could be put in the laws' category of
mutiny where Englishmen in a position similar to the colonists'
might use capital punishment. It was not, then, necessary to pass
a law, since even according to the charter they might use or ignore
the laws of England "as seemed best." A later development in
Smith's case, however, gave greater evidence of the autonomy of
Maryland law. Shortly before his execution Smith asked to see a
clergyman. "Clergy could not be allowed in this crime," the president said, "and if it might, yet now it was demanded too late after
judgement."[5] The assemblymen decided differently and had their
way. As judges they allowed the spiritual ministrations, and as
legislators they passed a law which would recognize this right for
Englishmen in the future.

These are examples of the way the assemblymen, under the
guiding spirit of religious liberty, interpreted the charter and their
new legal status. "There was a tendency to refer to the laws of
England so far as applicable,"[6] one authority says; but this was
not an obligation. Richard B. Morris speaks in general of, "the
failure of the colonists to formulate a definite theory as to the
extent of the transplantation of the common law and of the application of English Statutes to the colonies."[7] Maryland was nota-
ble in that English law had to be specifically legislated by the
assembly in each instance. At the same time, we cannot help but
notice the guiding spirit of English common law in its regard for
the rights of Englishmen. As Fortesque, the fifteenth century jur-
ist, and other commentators after him declared, these rights de-

rived from the law of nature. Smith actually won his case for a clergyman on these grounds against the opposition of Leonard Calvert, president of the assembly. An exercise of religious liberty, then, could be based on natural law as well as on the status as a Christian referred to in the charter.

The liberality shown to an Englishman was likewise shown to the church as a moral person with important rights in the Smith case. There was another instance confirming this in these early years of the colony. As property holders, Fathers Copley and White were expected to attend the assembly meetings. We do not know if either had attended the 1635 sessions. In the second session we note that they asked to be excused, as any colonists might do for a good reason. There is evidence that some legal arrangement eventually freed them permanently from this political function.[8] This was what the clergymen wanted, and it attested to their intention to use only spiritual means to fulfill their priestly office. From the state's standpoint, it was making a concession in favor of religion and the liberty necessary for fostering its growth.

There were other harmonious adjustments of rights. Clerical diplomatists were not unknown in Europe and they were even found among the Canadian French missionaries of this time. These missionaries were sometimes compromised when the provincial government urged a priest who had successfully evangelized a tribe to negotiate a policy favorable to French interests, which were often basically commercial. Governor Calvert once put a missionary, Father Rigbie, in a similar position with the Patuxent Indians.[9] Some tribe members had engaged in marauding English livestock, and the governor sought the easiest way of bringing the culprits to justice. He asked Father Rigbie to deliver a warrant of arrest and help in the apprehension. The assembly again showed a sensibility which Leonard Calvert lacked and came to the assistance of the clergyman. A law was passed to avert any such employment in the future. One more precedent was thus added to shape the distinctive contour of church-state relations in Maryland.

THE ASSEMBLY'S VICTORY

The burgeoning young colony was now moving ahead with its democratic spirit, expanding self-government and settling matters of freedom with great liberality. The Proprietor, Lord Baltimore, was kept informed, and he did not always like what he heard: laws already on the books, his brother the governor a mere functionary president of the assembly that passed them—this body that was to "advise and assent" to his own determinations. Within two years after the first assembly had adjourned, the proprietor had a letter in the hands of Governor Leonard Calvert instructing him how he was to proceed with this recalcitrant, precocious child. In a commission dated April 15, 1637, Lord Baltimore stated: "We . . . constitute . . . said Leonard Calvert to be our Chancellor, Chief Justice, and Chief Magistrate within our said Province . . . executing . . . all . . . things whatsoever, which belong to the establishing and governing of a good and happy commonwealth. . . ." As for the assembly, "We . . . give our said Lieutenant . . . absolute authority; . . . [it] shall be by him dissolved, at all or any other time or times, when and as often as he shall think fit; [or] to call and summon one."[10]

So equipped, the governor could deal with any future law-making. Lord Baltimore also had a categorical solution for the problem which past transactions of the assembly created for his proprietary powers. "We do disassent unto all the laws by them heretofore or at any time made within our said Province, and do hereby declare them to be void." With the ground cleared he told the governor that he would soon have in the hands of the secretary of the council and the assembly a copy of such laws as he judged good for the colony. Leonard Calvert would then convene the assembly in order to give it the privilege of assenting to these laws.

The first of the year, Governor Calvert addressed himself to the task which his brother imposed on him. According to the law passed at the first assembly, a session was to be held in that year, 1638, so that the governor was actually only carrying out an assembly order. On January 25, business got under way with a reading of the draft of Baltimore's code of laws. Each act of the code was discussed and heated controversy developed. The governor was involved in a two-pronged attack: opposition to the laws themselves and to Baltimore's denial of assembly authority. Calvert almost immediately lost the support of his chief council members, and Captain Thomas Cornwallis was emerging from the debate as the leader of the opposition. In the interim between the meetings of the 25th and the 29th, the two parties that took shape rallied their supporters and planned their strategy. The practice at these first assemblies was for absent freemen to give their vote to some attending member, but not necessarily with any instruction or limitation on the representative, called a proxy. Important men like Leonard Calvert, John Lewger and Thomas Cornwallis had been given several proxies. Calculations had to be in terms of voting done on this basis.

At the second meeting, on the 29th, the governor began to move for a vote, while Cornwallis fought for a delay. The latter hoped that a greater number of freemen would be in attendance in the coming meetings and the results under these conditions would be safer than with the large number of proxies that prevailed on the 29th. Cornwallis could not get agreement among his followers and the assembly determined by a good margin to begin voting on the code of Baltimore. On this procedure issue, Lewger and the governor, together with their proxies, polled an impressive majority. When the voting on the code began, however, Cornwallis found growing support for his move to reject the laws of Baltimore. At the final tally the governor and Lewger stood alone, the only present members who approved the code. All the others had voted with Cornwallis for a combined total of thirty-seven votes, including proxies. Between them the two members of the opposition had but twelve proxies. In spite of all the authority his commission gave him, the governor had failed to impress the assembly.

With the proprietor's laws defeated, the question was immediately asked from the floor "what laws the Province should be governed by"? "They might do well," some said, "to agree upon some laws." At this proposal the governor and president, Leonard Calvert, sprang to his feet in opposition, "denying any such power to be in the house."[11] Cornwallis immediately countered with what he considered to be the power of the house according to English tradition and law. By inherited parliamentary privilege the Maryland Assembly had the right to initiate legislation for the making of laws, and Cornwallis was determined to fight for this right. If Cornwallis should win, the governor realized that as agent of the proprietor he was not supreme in his authority over the assembly.

Leonard Calvert must certainly have been prepared for the outcome that now confronted him. Perhaps he had previously told his brother, the proprietor, what might be expected. Leonard knew that he would have to compromise and that his brother could not object once the whole encounter was fully narrated to him. The governor could not ask for another code from the proprietor, for the likelihood of rejection again would mean added delay with no solution resulting. Surrounded by these considerations, the governor had to sit in silence while it "was propounded that the house would consider some laws to be sent up to the Lord Proprietor." As president of the assembly, but with vanquished tone, he "advised that they would choose some committees to prepare the draught . . . and then the house would meet for confirming them. . . ."[12] The assembly agreed and selected him as a member of the committee. Cornwallis, however, received the largest vote for a place on the committee, and Lewger, who had advised the proprietor and governor on the rejected code, was denied committee membership. All of this was evidence that the assembly wanted to have the majority view dominate the new draft of laws.

The governor, however, would not yet give up. He seems to have recovered some influence in the committee which he did not have before the assembly. He may have warned the committee-men of the interminable process of repeal of laws, for the proprie-tor too could reject laws which the assembly was preparing to draft. Perhaps the original code of the proprietor could be modi-fied. Compromise, after all, was the temper of English politics. The heated debate of the assembly may not have given the code a fair chance. In this way the committeemen, with the exception of Cornwallis, were won over to the governor's view. The com-mittee thus reported to the assembly: "There was found a great deal of misunderstanding of them [Baltimore's code] among the freemen which made them refuse." The assembly agreed to con-sider the code again, upon this recommendation of the committee. For procedure the assemblymen agreed to read and discuss each section of the code on three different occasions before voting, which seemed to the advantage of the governor. In the final vote, however, the governor stood very much alone as the assembly proceeded to reject the proprietor's code once again.

As defeat was closing in on Leonard Calvert, he made one final sally in which he encountered once again his arch-opponent, Cap-tain Cornwallis. The governor recommended adjournment after the second defeat of Baltimore's code. This seemed proper, he explained, "until the laws which they would propound to the lord proprietor were made ready." Continuing this lead he ex-plained that "some would take care of [such laws] and in the meantime the company might attend their other business." Corn-wallis detected the ruse and demanded to know why the assembly should be adjourned. With the vexation of a defeated man the governor answered that he "would be accountable to no man for his adjourning it." But Cornwallis was more interested in knowing who the "some" were who "would take care of" drawing up the laws. He did not want their choice left to the governor. "A committee might be appointed," Cornwallis proposed, "that should take charge of preparing the laws until the house met again."[13] It was a wise maneuver, bypassing discussion of the governor's power to adjourn; and the governor could not object to the voting that settled the personnel of the committee. Cornwallis had won a parliamentary victory and proceeded to gain the greatest majority vote of any of the members who were then elected by the assembly for the second committee to draft a new code of laws.

This closing scene was reminiscent of Charles I's clash with Parliament. In spirit and principle, also, Cornwallis was in the role of those who stood over John Lackland at Runnymede demanding the rights that became the Magna Charta. He had carried forward a tradition that had derived from it and gave this tradition further growth on the widening frontier of Maryland. Persons had pointed to popular voice in government as a remedy for tyranny, and Bellarmine had established its foundation in the law of nature. The Marylanders, however, had created a practical expression of the idealism of these two men when they successfully defended their own notion of what their assembly should be. The assembly promised to be a weapon against oppression from above by the proprietor and king; beneath it were the people to whose welfare it was sensitive because the people chose its members. The Marylanders were truly striving to construct a citadel of freedom in the assembly they were building.

V. THEIR RIGHTS AND LIBERTIES

The assembly began to receive various acts which the committee offered as a basis of Maryland law in place of the code of Lord Baltimore. Leonard Calvert turned to the distasteful task of making a governor's report to the proprietor. "The body of laws you sent over by Mr. Lewger," he wrote on April 25, 1638, "I endeavored to have passed by the assembly at Maryland but could not effect. . . ." He was hardly in a position to criticize his brother's code, but he was evidently impressed by the assembly debate which suggested what future laws should be. "There were so many things unsuitable to the people's good," he candidly said of the code, "and no way conducing to your profit." Leonard Calvert was saying politely that he was a good judge of things in Maryland and that laws could best be designed in the atmosphere of the colony. He reassured the proprietor of the laws that were being passed: "I am persuaded they will appear unto you to provide both for your honor and profit as much as those you sent us. . . ."[1] The governor was recommending conciliation, anticipating any possible intransigence by the proprietor when he was presented with the Maryland laws.

Thomas Cornwallis was in a different position. He was an important customer of the proprietor, a heavy investor in land and trade in Maryland. The colony was looking to his military leadership against the Indians and the threat of the Virginians under Claiborne. He also felt the lingering glow of his victory in the

93

assembly and a passionate determination to defend the ground that was won. With these dispositions Cornwallis sat down and wrote a forthright letter which would arrive in England together with the mild report of the governor. The code was not "for the people's good," as the governor himself had said, and was even "prejudicial to our honors and freedom," Cornwallis boldly stated. "We are exposed," he wrote of the code, "to a remedy-less suffering of all disgraces and insolencies that either the passion or the malice of succeeding governors shall please to put upon us."[2] Having won the right to initiate legislation, Cornwallis was determined to protect the future colony against tyranny by the written laws of his assembly. Baltimore's code did not give this assurance.

THE INHABITANTS OF THIS PROVINCE

With the code in front of them, Cornwallis and the other members of the committee set about drafting the series of acts which would come before the assembly and eventually be embodied in the ordinance completed and passed in 1639. What was so objectionable in the code? What threatened the "people's good"? First of all, it was too long, according to the committeemen. Much of it elaborated the charter and employed its traditional phraseology, which could be interpreted broadly in favor of the colonists. "Be it therefore enacted and ordained by the said Lord Proprietor . . . with the advice, assent and approbation of the freemen," read the first act of Baltimore's code. The assemblymen could hardly have been offended by this, particularly when Baltimore stated his belief that the Maryland Assembly should have "like power . . . as the House of Commons . . . had used or enjoyed . . . or of right ought to have use or enjoy."[3] The assemblymen were especially pleased to see Baltimore explicitly provide that the assembly should by law convene every three years. His provisions that lords of the manor be distinct from the freemen in the assembly, however, smacked too much of an unrealistic feudal mentality.

When Baltimore began to describe his proprietary powers the assembly became alarmed. "All acts," said one critical passage, "shall be of force until the Lord Proprietor shall signify his disassent to the same. . . ." While this implied the power to initiate legislation, it denied the assembly the right definitively to make the laws which governed them. In a passage on felonies Baltimore legislated against anyone "exercising within the province any jurisdiction or authority which ought to be derived from the Lord Proprietor without lawful power or commission from or under him." This position of supremacy over Maryland law thus carried over into the realm of personal rights with the same spirit of infringement. Cornwallis revolted when he read that none shall be imprisoned nor dispossessed except "according to the laws of this province, saving to the Lord Proprietor and his heirs all his rights and prerogatives by reason of his domination and seigniory over this province and the people of the same." Such reservations on the rights of Englishmen were intolerable. There were others. In Baltimore's act for the liberties of the people, he cast some doubt on the natural rights of non-Christians. He explicitly excluded slaves from any benefits of this act. All liberties were to be according to common law and the statute law of England in general, so that laws and ordinances of the colony must explicitly rule otherwise in each specific case in order to annul the force of English laws. This would have narrowed the broad privileges of the charter. Oppressively overhanging the code's act for the liberties of the people was the expression of the proprietor's "domination and seigniory over this province and the people."[4] When Cornwallis read the elaborate provision for courts of admiralty, chancery, county, etc., he was provoked to the rhetoric that won the debate in the assembly and found its way into the letter he sent to Lord Baltimore. With the code as a starting point, Cornwallis had a clear idea of what laws should go into the ordinance on which his committee was working. The other members, even the governor, began to see the matter his way.

The committeemen turned from the code to their own task. Brief and simple acts began to emerge; Baltimore's code took up forty pages in our printed version, the ordinance but a few. The rights of Marylanders were set forth without any of the reservations which Baltimore had tried to impose. "All the inhabitants of this province," read one act, "shall have all their rights and liberties according to the Great Charter of England." There was no limitation of Christian and non-Christian, nor subservience of colonists to proprietor. We find here that general reference to the rights of Englishmen which many writers of the time found to be derived from the citizen's nature as man. There was no complicated description of a system of courts to maintain these rights. There was only the simple and direct charge given every magistrate and government official to "cause right and justice to be done in all causes civil . . . according to the laws or laudable usages of this province. . . ."[5] Yet the citizen could draw on the rich tradition of experience in human rights to be found in the common law of England, but without any enslavement to specific statute laws which may on occasion in the past have violated the spirit of human freedom found in this tradition. English statute laws would have to be specifically voted in order to become operative in Maryland.

The drafters eliminated the hovering overlord found in the code's version of the rights of the people, but they had a more delicate operation to perform in their "Act for Establishing the House of Assembly and the Laws to be Made Therein." They had to accept the charter phraseology with its saving element of ambiguity when they wrote of the "full, free and absolute power and authority of the Lord Proprietor of this Province to make and ordain any laws appertaining to the state of this province by and with the advice, assent and approbation of the freemen of the same."[6] But this was saying more than the charter, since the added word, *approbation,* is more forceful than *assent.* Moreover, when Lord Baltimore acquiesced in the ordinance that was drafted in 1639, he accepted the democratic procedure of initiating legislation, which the assembly used in arriving at the ordinance. In other words, "the advice, assent and approbation of the freemen" meant that the assembly had to approve any legislation the proprietor might propose before it became law. In addition, the assembly could initiate legislation itself. This was a step considerably beyond the petition of rights which fought only for the privilege of approbation and not initiation.

This giant stature of the assembly is reflected in the very first act of the proposed ordinance: "All acts and ordinances assented unto and approved by the said house or by the major part of the persons assembled and afterward assented unto by the Lieutenant General [Governor] in the name of the said Lord Proprietor . . . shall be adjudged and established for laws to all with the same force and effect as if the said Lord Proprietor and all the freemen of this Province were personally present and did assent to and approve the same."[7] The governor, as president of the assembly, might oppose a piece of legislation and then be compelled to give his official signature to the bill because it had won a majority of the assembly. This is what actually happened in the case of the ordinance itself. Could the governor pass the bill on to the proprietor without signing it, thereby obstructing its passage? Conceivably, but we are dealing with English institutions where precedent is so important. If the proprietor *did not* override the assembly, in time it would be a matter of acceptance that he *could not.* This seems to be the historic nature of the sacrifice Baltimore was making in his compromise with the Maryland Assembly in its sessions of 1638 and 1639. The king himself would experience the consequences 137 years later when he defied the colonial tradition which such precedents as Maryland's had created.

Cornwallis began to feel assured. The committee had contrived

a "remedy" against the "suffering . . . that . . . the malice of
succeeding Governors shall please to put upon us."[8] Laws of
Maryland's making put down on paper the "honors and freedom"
he cherished so much. Moreover, in the assembly thus defined by
these laws, Marylanders had a living guardian of the "inhabitants
of this province." Perhaps Bellarmine and Persons might have
recognized these beginnings as the instruments of that democratic government which their principles implied. The assembly
became the guardian of the political order which would be the
benefactor of conscience and simplify the problem of church-state
relations.

The thorniest part of Baltimore's code was its fourth "Act for
Maintaining the Lord Proprietor's Title to the Lands of the Province." Before this time the official document, Conditions of Plantation, set down the property and commercial agreement between
the proprietor and his colonist. It was more in the nature of a
private contract between two parties and was distinct from the
charter, which was like a constitution establishing civil authority.
By this act in his code, Baltimore tended to confuse the two
realms, the commercial and civil. It would be easy for him in the
future under benefit of such a law to usurp civil authority in promoting what might be founded only on a private contract.

The first point Baltimore made in his act was that any land
which a colonist acquired must be on the basis of a contract with
himself. The theory of this must have been clear to any Englishman before he came to America. Territory in North America had
been claimed in the name of the king who had relinquished title
to the Maryland territory in favor of Lord Baltimore and his heirs.
In practice, however, the colonists on their arrival saw the governor conduct matters on a different basis. He assumed that the Indians owned the territory and had to negotiate with them for
rights. Could not an individual colonist also engage in such transactions? The citizen's title to such land could not be questioned
any more than a purchase of land in France. Baltimore said in

his act, however, that he alone could negotiate for land; anyone else acquired it for the proprietor. The theory of proprietary rights was not entirely real, then, with the result that one could argue with it. The fact was that the missionaries had been given land by the Indians and were becoming dependent upon it for future work among the Indians and colonists. Were they as Englishmen deprived of the right to acquire title from these foreign holders? Did their status as clergymen of a universal church whose interests were dependent upon such temporal support give them immunity from Baltimore's provision in the code?

The committee held back from this controversy, but saw to it that Baltimore's version did not enter into the ordinance, even though they necessarily had to make some allusion to the proprietary nature of the Maryland territory. They dealt with the simplest case in their provision: "If any goods be within the province without any challenging the same and having right thereunto, the lieutenant general and council shall appoint how the same shall be employed."[9] This surely was a more realistic, if more complicated, way of proceeding, providing for a settlement of difficult cases by judicial procedures. At the same time the recommendation favored the rights of Englishmen in acquiring land.

The average colonist felt the real pinch on his freedom in passages of Baltimore's code regarding trade with the Indians. The committee and assembly became intransigent in their opposition, and one can easily see why. Baltimore would forbid all contact with the Indians without a license from his own agent. The purpose was plainly commercial although Baltimore attempted to put the matter on the basis of peace and security for the colony, which might reasonably demand supervision of indiscriminate dealings with the Indians. The Marylanders, however, felt that they had paid dearly for their land and that trading activity was a major means of making good their investment. They wanted the greatest freedom for themselves and feared the monopoly which Baltimore's provision was setting up. The movement of the missionaries might also be restricted by such an explicit and narrow law. Here again the whole matter was more proper to the Conditions of Plantation than to a code of public law. The proprietor should have seen to it in his private contracts with the settlers.

Baltimore had become unrealistic in his remote position. He showed no appreciation of the temper of the colonists when he had recourse to the privy council in England before he drew up his code. He then dictated to the assembly using the council's authority to back up his own interpretation as to what his rights were in land titles and trade with the Indians. Perhaps he began to understand the Marylanders, however, when he read his brother's letter of 1638. His awakening was more thorough when he received the ordinance of 1639 and found no mention of his proposed control over dealings with the Indians. The inhabitants were beginning boldly to insist on their rights and liberties.

HOLY CHURCH WITHIN THIS PROVINCE

Cornwallis wrote to the proprietor with great feeling for the colonists' political freedom, but he had an even greater concern. In the same letter he wrote: "I will rather sacrifice myself and all I have in defense of God's honor and his Church's right, than willingly consent to anything that may not stand with the conscience of a real Catholic."[10] Baltimore's code awakened this grave alarm and made Cornwallis intent on securing the rights of the church in the laws his committee was preparing for the ordinance. As described previously, the committeemen dealt with peripheral matters of church liberty when they omitted Baltimore's provision for control of contact with the Indians and when they left to the courts controverted land rights, in which the missionaries were sure to be involved. The ordinance, however, was to be a fundamental set of laws and needed more than these token gestures of respect for the church. The maintenance of tolerance demanded it, as well as protection of the state. Because Maryland had professed by *Objections Answered* to give a lesson in these matters, fundamental principles had to be formulated, though details might be left to the spirit of religious freedom that had already made such a promising beginning.

The committeemen had to become philosophers of government. Cornwallis, however, demurred from this role. He urged Lord Baltimore to see that what was decided upon was approved by "learned and religious divines."[11] The other members of the committee, however, must have attacked on their own initiative passages which touched on the rights of the church. John Lewger, secretary of the assembly and committee member, tried to formulate the theoretical nature of the problem which the code brought up. In his own letter to Lord Baltimore about the time that Cornwallis was writing, Lewger revealed the difficulty of fitting the Maryland situation into any familiar church-state scheme found in Europe. Baltimore was a Catholic prince, but under a heretical king. The privileges of Durham, however, gave him great autonomy. Must the proprietor's agents proceed entirely on this basis to settle matters after the manner of a Catholic country such as Spain? But there were new situations in a colonial structure and to deal with them one had to determine, according to Lewger, whether the state derived its authority from the church or the church from the state. He was particularly preoccupied with such practices of Catholic countries as "exemptions of the clergy for their persons, lands, goods, tenants, domestics, or privileges of sanctuary to their houses, or churches, etc. . . ."[12] If these things were "due to them of divine right by immediate grant from Christ to his Church . . . princes becoming Christians were instantly obliged in conscience to allow and confirm those exemptions. . . ." Thomas More had revolted against this absolutist explanation of the rights of the church which implied dependence of the church on the state. The signers of the Remonstrance would also have objected to Lewger's equating "liberties and exemptions"; for the church must always have its liberty, and exemptions are but one of many means of protecting liberty.

When we consider the background of Lewger we see that he was not a good spokesman for the tradition which we have been considering. He had only been a convert to Catholicism for a short time before coming to Maryland. Perhaps this prevented him from seeing the third alternative which Suárez and Bellarmine saw in explaining the origin of rights and authority. Unlike Cardinal Allen, Lewger did not seize the immediate insight of Gelasius which established the autonomy of each authority, temporal and spiritual. The Christian prince does not derive his civil authority from the church but, as Bellarmine instructed James I, from the people, thus founding it in the nature of man. The church had its authority long before the king existed or even before there was an England, as More had said so dramatically. Lewger did not identify himself with this line of reasoning. Therefore, he could not conclude that each authority should pursue its own distinct purpose, the one spiritual, the other temporal; that each was entitled to the means which conditions in Maryland would decide to be appropriate.

Lewger may have been too much a partisan of the proprietor to see the reality of the situation. With the assembly functioning as it did, Baltimore was not a Christian prince playing the benefactor of the church in feudal style. Like Baltimore in his code, Lewger was too intent on being guided by what was done in other countries. He was not gripped by the creative bent which inspired the assemblymen and which led them, in rejecting Baltimore's code, to devise an approach based on a broad general understanding of the growing Catholic tradition in England, together with a practical grasp of the challenging opportunity of an infant colony.

The wisest thing that the committeemen could do would be to state the rights of the church in the broadest and most fundamental form, so that relations with the state might proceed on a flexible basis, adapted to the unique conditions and developments of the New World. Perhaps one needed to be on the scene at St. Mary's City to discern this. The committeemen in their draft began to move in this direction by a simple initial formula: "Holy Church within this Province shall have all her rights and liberties." They were familiar with a long line of charters which went back to the Magna Charta, where mention was made of the rights of the church together with the rights of Englishmen. Baltimore himself had used some of these consecrated formulas, but he had complicated matters when he added "immunities" to "rights and liberties."[13] In doing this he was saddling the infant colony with the legal usage which European countries had given to the word. The committeemen refused to suggest the consequences which immunities implied and which John Lewger had outlined in his letter to Baltimore. Hence the act which they devised passed into the ordinance in a form which adhered more closely to the Magna Charta.

We find a textual difficulty in the record which the *Proceedings of the Assembly* gives us of the ordinance's "Act for the Church Liberties"; and out of the discussion which it provokes we come upon the deeper implications of its terse statement. The uncorrected version has, "Holy *Churches* within this province shall have all *her* rights and Liberties." Where are we to put the error of the scrivener, in *Churches* or in *her*? There seems little doubt that the singular was intended. This was the Magna Charta form and this is what we find in the *Proceedings of the Assembly* for 1640 when the act is repeated. The scrivener may have had the seventeenth-century form of the possessive singular in mind with the intention of using the passive voice, "Holy Churches rights and liberties shall be maintained. . . ." The writer was distracted from this construction. We might simply explain that he would be more likely to make a mechanical error with the ending of a word than with choice of a completely different word such as *her* for *their*.

This textual consideration comes up largely because some writers have centered their explanation of toleration in the plural form of church. The assemblymen, according to them, were trying to

adapt the phrasing of the traditional English charters, but between the ordinance and these charters stood the disruption of
European religious unity with the Protestant revolt. There was
not one church but many. The assembly intended that Marylanders of whatever faith or church should enjoy the traditional liberties of these charters according to a new adaptation to this historic
change. All churches should enjoy the rights and liberties ac-
corded the one church before Henry VIII's break with Rome.

This supposition, however, is too simple for the seventeenth-
century Englishman's situation, whether in England or America.
He had a living memory of religious unity in Europe from which
he was not many years removed. It would be safe to say that each
sect believed that there was but one church. Diversity arose only
from disagreement about the outward form of the church: and
all were bent upon winning converts to their view of what that
form should be. To the Anglican, for example, this meant the
proper order of worship (the *Book of Common Prayer*) and the
king as head of the church. It was on all sides a question of dealing with the recalcitrant and heterodox. The legislators seemed to
be clearly aware that there were many views about the true nature
of the church, and did not, with their brief statement, pretend to
remove by force of law any of this diversity. The singular, *church,*
was indeed ambiguous, but it was an honest ambiguity.

Where, then, did the legislators of the ordinance provide for
freedom of conscience, which defenders of the plural form have
found in this passage on the liberties of the church? This question
has an ill-advised supposition. Individual freedom is not likely to
be found in a passage which purports to deal with a group of
persons such as the church, technically termed a *moral person*. It
is true that if the church is free, individuals will indirectly gain
certain freedom as members. But such an indirect approach leads
to the conclusion that one must become a member of a church
before he can as an individual win toleration and freedom of conscience. Nor is this reasoning faithful to the understandings of

Englishmen. According to their tradition, as More witnessed, the individual's rights to freedom of conscience were distinct from the right of a group, or moral person, such as the church. This distinction between the two sources of rights is found in the Magna Charta. Faithful to this tradition, the committeemen provided two distinct acts for liberty, one for the individual, the other for the church. In the broad provision of the first, "The inhabitants of this province shall have all their rights and liberties according to the Great Charter," we should place the individual's right to freedom of conscience. In the second we find recognition of the higher spiritual society with its autonomous functions as a moral person.

The committeemen made other changes in the code of Baltimore in matters related to the "Act for Church Liberties." We have already discussed the code's "Act for the Liberties of the People" and its employment of the phrase, "being Christian." Baltimore may not have intended to exclude non-Christians from the traditional rights of Englishmen. The phrase evidently was written with the force of a consideration added to the status of Englishmen, a further motive for respecting rights. There was nevertheless danger of confusion. When the ordinance omitted the phrase it acted consistently with its position on the rights of the individual as distinct from those of the church. One need not be a Christian to benefit from the "Act for the Rights of the People."[14] At the same time, the omission of "being Christian" was not a secularist's oversimplification, for the "Act for the Liberties of the Church" had the state recognize the superior spiritual society.

Baltimore's code gave rise to another difficulty. He legislated against sacrilege and sorcery and stated that: "It shall be adjudged a felony within this Province to commit idolatry, which is the worshipping a false God or to commit blasphemy which is accursing or wicked speaking of God. . . ."[15] He imposed the harshest penalties and called the attention of justices of the peace to these matters. The whole passage suggested the medieval prince who assumed personal guardianship of his subject's spiritual welfare and acted as the secular arm of the church. Under the pressure of Calvinistic theology, such laws as these found growing support in the England of Calvert's day. The Puritan theory of them, however, derived less from the notion of feudal government than from the economy of the chosen people of the Old Testament.

The ordinance drafters sensed the explosive nature of these provisions for the colony—perhaps because they understood better than Calvert the colony's pluralistic form and characteristic toleration. They could recall the European history of such laws as Baltimore had written. Closer to them they saw the civil courts of the Massachusetts Bay Colony building up a casuistry which dealt with an array of religious topics. Civil magistrates became judges of an individual's guilt of blasphemy and determined the nature of idolatry and sorcery. In the light of what they had drawn up for the ordinance the committeemen saw that such matters were essentially spiritual, and proper judgment for the church and her ministers. At the same time, their act for felonies took adequate account of the temporal aspects of incidents developing from these religious matters. "The lieutenant general or any one of the council," it read, "shall or may command and appoint all power and means necessary or conducive to the apprehending of felons or keeping the peace."[16] Thus the assembly designated no religious felonies as such. Any civil disorder which came about from the religious matters Baltimore had mentioned would be dealt with in accord with the laws for "keeping the peace." The temptation was to name religious situations which might give rise to disorder. But the committeemen saw that once they were named the magistrate must begin defining religious matters. This Gelasian reserve kept the distinction of church and state clear.

Baltimore must have expected that part of his code which

brought forth an oath of allegiance also to be rejected by the assemblymen. He proposed a version that had none of the most objectionable features of the oath of James I; but even to broach the matter would bring a feeling of distress. Perhaps the committeemen coupled Baltimore's oath with his provision for treason. The oath obliged the colonist "to disclose and make known to his Majesty, his heirs and lawful successors all treason and traitorous conspiracies. . . ." In another place Baltimore declared it to be treasonous to "adhere to any foreign prince or state being a professed and declared enemy of his Majesty in any practice or attempt against his said majesty."[17] The colonist's memory must have rebelled against all of this, and in his hopes for the future of the colony, which he appreciated better than the proprietor, he turned to a better solution. Many Maryland Catholics remembered that their spiritual head, the pope, had been designated by English rulers a foreign prince and enemy of the crown, thus branding his English adherents as traitors. They had also seen the malice that the practice of informing had bred among Englishmen. Neither of these matters could go into the fundamental law that the ordinance was to become. The Marylanders would wait, and perhaps a suitable oath could be devised to give outward expression to the loyalty of the small group of settlers who knew one another well enough safely to allow treason to reveal itself.

The drafters of the ordinance solved the problem which another part of the Baltimore code presented when they simply omitted for the time being any consideration of marriage contracts. "All causes matrimonial," the code read,

foreasmuch as concerns the trial of covenants and contracts and the punishment of faults committed against the same and . . . clandestine marriage without banns thrice published or bond entered in court, . . . for which any certain punishment is appointed by the laws of this province or by the Common Law of England, shall be heard and determined finally by and before the chief justices of the province for

the time being or and before such other commissioner or commissioners as the Lord Proprietor of this province or the Lieutenant General shall authorize to hear and determine the same.[18]

To the mind of the assemblymen this must have seemed an awk-
ward law for a delicate matter of church-state relations. By his
clause, "foreasmuch as . . ." Baltimore does, however, seem to
recognize the exclusively spiritual aspects of these matters which
concerned the church.

These, then, were the details of the laws which the Maryland
Assembly passed during its sessions of 1638 and 1639. At the end
of the *Proceedings of the Assembly* for 1639, they were all brought
together in their brief and concise form to compose the ordinance.
It was then summarily stated that the assembly gave its assent to
all these laws and that the governor signed the ordinance in the
name of the proprietor. The assembly then adjourned. There were
some minor additions to the ordinance the following year, but in
the laws of 1639 the Marylander could find all his rights and liberties.

VI. THOSE PROFESSING BELIEF

MARYLAND had its basic set of laws. Its own inhabitants had fashioned them according to their own mind and the environment which inspired them to apply inherited principles. What meaning did they take on for the different religious persuasions which were planted and grew in Maryland? This, in a sense, introduces another story, a sequel to the one we have been telling. By way of epilogue, however, we can find suggestions of what this sequel might be in broad outline. Here and there in the record of the times we find ripples on the surface which reveal the vitality of the wellsprings of 1639, indicating the persistence of a tradition.

CATHOLICS, PURITANS, QUAKERS, JEWS

We can see signs of the Catholic adjustment in a controversy between Baltimore and the Jesuits in the decade following the ordinance. A letter which Father Copley wrote to Lord Baltimore at the time the assembly was criticizing his code told of church-state issues and portended the personal conflict between the two parties over land holding. Copley told Baltimore that he was greatly distressed that while immunities were referred to in the "Act for Church Liberties" in his code, no specific provision was made to free the clergy from civil courts nor to do the same for laymen who were employed residents on church land.[1] The ordinance gave more dissatisfaction to him since it entirely omitted the term *immunities*. Copley thought within the framework of existing European church-state settlements. Since the proprietor was a Catholic, Maryland should follow the practices of Spain, or something similar which expressed the devotedness of the Christian prince. The ordinance, however, made it strikingly clear to Copley that such a notion of union between church and state the assembly did not share.

Copley did not take the broad approach of the assembly to this matter; and, as time went on, the discussion with Baltimore brought this out. Baltimore became determined to resist Copley's claim to land which the Indians had given the Jesuits. Copley invoked certain church legislation against Baltimore, attempting to establish immunity from confiscation for this land because it was church property. According to the Bull cited, confiscation of church property carried the penalty of excommunication.[2] Baltimore's case, however, was that the Jesuits did not have legal title to the land. Starting from this point he reasoned that his title came from legitimate temporal authority and no clergyman could deprive him of it. The Bull the Jesuit referred to did not seem to apply to Baltimore's case since it was designed to prevent the arbitrary confiscation of land to which the church had long held clear title. Copley's grievance, perhaps, was more with the civil nature of a palatinate as described in the charter, which had an unrealistic element in its notion of original property ownership in North America.

Baltimore did reflect more of the Old World than the New in his code, but he made it forcefully clear that he did not accept Copley's suggestion that a union of church and state found with accompanying practices in Catholic countries should be enforced in Maryland. In connection with his letter, Baltimore expressed a view, which was similar to More and Gelasius, that clergymen and even a bishop himself played the role of temporal citizens, subject to civil rulers. On the supposition that he had legal title to all Maryland property, Baltimore said that he was determined to defend his right in such a temporal matter against any colonist, even if he be a clergyman. He expressed the greatest surprise at Copley's plea for immunity for laymen on church property.[3] His father had signed the Remonstrance of Grievances without qualms of conscience; Cecil Calvert had the same mind in the matter, that the rights of the church do not demand the same elaboration in one country that they might have in another.

The dispute over Jesuit land titles eventually came to the provincial of the English mission for settlement. The Calverts had evidently been on the best of terms with the men who held this office. Father Blount had encouraged George Calvert in his grand design for a palatinate; and his successor, with whom Cecil now had to deal, gave promise of an amicable settlement. It was none other than the great-grandson of Sir Thomas More, Father Henry More, with whom he had to deal. More seemed possessed of the same broad understandings of church-state principles which had grown up among English Catholics from the days of his distinguished forebear. Like the chancellor, Henry More had felt the harsh blow of religious persecution. He once wrote of his 1628 arrest in the following manner: "The house was surrounded about nine o'clock in the morning. The officers broke in and searched the house from top to bottom. They seized the Rector, who was hidden in a cave underground with the sacred vessels and altar furniture, and other fathers: others were caught in various places. They were conducted to the different prisons and tried. . . ."[4]

Henry More had his own problem with the English oaths. Out of his experience, he once advised a friend:

In our resolutions and discourses concerning matters now most in agitation, we do not swerve from the best and safest and necessary ways which hitherto all ours . . . have ever walked, not admitting in things so nearly concerning faith and religion, any such subtle ways or evasions as the love of the world only can suggest, and cannot proceed from the spirit of God and truth.

From the days of James I's Oath, modified oaths had not lost their dangerous ambiguities. More felt that in taking such oaths one was professing Protestantism, an act of hypocrisy for any believing Catholic. "Every Christian heart and tongue," More concluded, "cannot but abhor unfeignedly to profess toward another profession which is not Catholic. . . ."[5] As *Objections Answered* had reasoned, it would not be the part of a wise state to breed such hypocrisy. The relief which Maryland gave from this condition must have been highly esteemed by More, with the result that he saw the wisdom of the ordinance's reserve and reverence in religious matters, which was the logical expression of the Maryland spirit of law.

More reflected in other ways the tradition found in Maryland. When the Bishop of Chalcedon aroused fear among English Catholics that he would establish all of the practices of Catholic countries, he took the side of Lord Baltimore and the others who signed the Remonstrance of Grievances. On another occasion he showed great liberality with the state in a mixed matter, when he gave favorable consideration to a protestation attached to an oath of 1641, in which Father White joined him. Liberty and private worship were promised to Catholics if they abstained from the belief that the pope could absolve from obedience to civil governors, that it was lawful to break an oath with heretics, or kill the censured and excommunicated. The spirit behind this acceptance may have been the Gelasian distinction of orders and the submission of bishops to princes in temporal matters. Though this was undoubtedly the mind of More, the protestation might have implied more than the two men intended, which was always the danger in the oath controversy. In these protestations the state implicitly acted the dangerous role with Catholics which it held in the Church of England; it attempted to define the powers of the pope and to settle a spiritual matter. The ordinance had, together with the early precedents of the colony, avoided this defect by its delicate sensibility and restraint in matters of religious liberty.

In the light of this it was not strange that More accepted the basic nature of Maryland church-state relations. Thus we cannot attribute to him and Father White the mentality which Father Copley reflected in his letter regarding immunities. This did not mean that the settlement of the land dispute was entirely to the satisfaction of More and the missionaries. The Jesuits had to relinquish title to the land which the Indians had given them and look to the future of their work without adequate means to support all their plans. Their case against Baltimore was not so much a matter of church-state relations as the obligation of Baltimore to the missionaries whom he encouraged as a private Catholic benefactor to come to America. More made no point of immunities in the final settlement and Baltimore had his way in the land dispute.

In the settlement More could look to the evident blessings the Catholic found in the Maryland arrangement and be assured. The Catholic had but a gnawing, unfulfilled desire ten years before; now in the truth of the new daylight he saw the reward Providence held out to him. Since 1634 he saw his faith begin to take on an external expression which the stifled conditions of England had never permitted. Catholics took pride in professing their faith. Many who had rejected it, or little understood it because of former repressive measures, now came to share the Catholic's esteem for it, and some in the freedom of the New World accepted it for the first time. Within the church, the luxury of public worship, of retreats for the laity in the *Spiritual Exercises* of St. Ignatius, of open conduct of religious instruction, were the first fruits of planting, and thanks to the ordinance, they promised to endure and multiply in due season. When the aborigines embraced the faith, as they began to do, the conquest of Christ and his Providence for his Church dramatized the splendor of the life of faith he had given the colonists.

A few years after the ordinance was signed, Puritans became noticeable among the residents of Maryland. Many of them had emigrated from Virginia because they had hoped for relief from the penalties their non-conformity brought them in a colony dominated by established Anglicanism. Maryland officials encouraged them. In some Puritan eyes, however, Baltimore was identified with Charles I, against whom they had serious grievances. Puritan opposition began to organize in 1642 in England when the first stages of the Civil War got under way. By 1644 Charles had suffered a damaging defeat at the battle of Marston Moor and the following year began to topple from the throne when the Puritans won the decisive battle of Naseby. In vain Charles conceded to Parliament in the hope of rallying Scots to his cause; but Cromwell defeated the Duke of Hamilton in the north and Parliament rejected any negotiation with the king. Parliament, in fact, proceeded the following year to the business of beheading its king.

This was a crucial period for Maryland, for Baltimore in vindicating his charter rights, and for the colonists in maintaining their tradition. As Puritans increased in numbers and their partisans won more power in England, the pressure on the Maryland government mounted. Baltimore appointed a Protestant governor, a token of his determination not to make religious persuasion a qualification for office, and a placating gesture to Puritan critics. But evidently among some, only a Puritan regime would do, or certainly a government purged of papists. The Virginian, Claiborne, tacking with the changing winds, decided to use a Puritan uprising to make good his land claims against Maryland, having failed to do so earlier. With the assistance of the Puritans he overthrew the Maryland government. Governor Leonard Calvert had been away from the colony at the time, but when he returned he was able to recover control. All of this did not prevent a growing ascendency of Puritan influence in the assembly. Puritans began to leave their mark, even if in a passing way, on Maryland law in ways which manifested a spirit quite different from what characterized the ordinance of 1639. This was particularly true of Puritan influence on the assembly of 1649.

In that year, however, Baltimore was able to work out a compromise to protect Catholics which resulted in a Toleration Act. Contrary to the thought of the ordinance, the Puritans inserted a passage similar to an act against disbelief written by the Puritan Parliament: "Whatsoever person . . . shall from henceforth . . . deny Our Saviour Jesus Christ to be the Son of God . . . shall be punished. . . ." Because of this characteristically Puritan position the ordinance basis of toleration had to be narrowed, apparently to the exclusion of Jews. Baltimore was able to have the following included in the Toleration Act: "No person . . . professing to believe in Jesus Christ, shall from henceforth be in any ways troubled . . . for or in respect of his or her religion nor in the free exercise thereof within this Province nor any way be compelled to the belief or exercise of any other religion against his will." In his charter and code, Baltimore did not seem to make acceptance of Christianity a condition for civil benefits and toleration; but in the Toleration Act the above passage expressly provided only for the Christian. In another part of the act we find a general provision for toleration on the broader basis of the right of a citizen, whatever his religious affiliation. The whole of this passage was reminiscent of *Objections Answered:* "Whereas the enforcing of conscience in matters of religion has frequently fallen out to be of dangerous consequence to those commonwealths where it has been practiced, and for the more quiet and peaceable government of this province, and the better to preserve mutual love and amity among the inhabitants thereof . . ."[6]—for these reasons penalties are set down against those who disparage another's religious belief. In the final analysis, the Toleration Act could in court be used in favor of the tradition which the ordinance embodied and which the instruction of Baltimore expressed in words similar to the last passage cited.

Throughout the Puritan period, Lord Baltimore skillfully maintained the palatinate status of Maryland and Catholics were the first to benefit from that status. We read of Thomas Matthews and Cuthbert Fenwick, who refused to take the oath of secrecy on religious grounds and were about to be excluded from the assembly by the Puritan majority. Fenwick then entered certain reservations in an offer to take the oath, which were also rejected. Whereupon he pleaded his case on the basis of the Toleration Act; the assembly reversed its former stand and explained that it did not intend to infringe freedom of conscience by prescribing the oath. The long practiced delicacy of past assemblies on such matters as well as the prestige of Baltimore explain the settlement. At a later date we find a Father Fitzherbert more directly appealing to the Maryland tradition and specifically to the ordinance.[7] From the court record it would seem that he had been engaging in street preaching and that complaints had led to charges against him. In the course of the case in 1662, Fitzherbert successfully pleaded benefit from the ordinance's "Act for Church Liberties," and then made good his claim that his conduct of the ministry did not bring any disturbance of the peace.[8]

Even before the Fitzherbert case, during the Puritan ascendency in 1658, two Quakers made their cases in a way similar to the above two incidents. Josias Cole and Thomas Thurston were charged with abstention from an oath and were said to "go on still to seduce many of the people unto erroneous and blasphemous tenets."[9] Then one of the Quakers responded that in being forced to take the oath "he is denied his liberty and the liberty of a subject." Both men claimed that there could be no question of law regarding belief, but only a matter of what concerns the public peace, before the court. When Thurston was banished, the court based its decision on the charge of peace disturbance. Eventually, with the passing of the Puritan majority, the assembly passed a law freeing Quakers from oaths in any form; but it is to the discredit of Baltimore and his policy of currying favor of the powers in England that he earlier took no action on William Penn's request for relief of Quakers at the time that it was made.

The irony of these events continued in an incident which involved a Jew and two Quakers, one of whom was Josias Cole. Jacob Lumbrozo apparently had no difficulty as a Jew in getting the legal recognition of a freeholder status and served for a time in the assembly. He even practiced law in Maryland. One day, however, he engaged in discussion of religion with Cole and Richard Preston, a prominent Puritan who had turned Quaker after the Stuart restoration in 1660. Preston had come from Virginia as a Puritan, served as speaker of the assembly in 1654, and was made commissioner under Governor Fuller. When Preston and Cole began to argue with Lumbrozo, they took offense at his denial that Christ was a divine person who had exercised miraculous powers. On the Quakers' evidence Lumbrozo was brought into court. "He had some talk with those persons," the record says in explaining Lumbrozo's stand, "and . . . answered to some particular demands they urged, and as to that of miracles done by magic (in the case of Christ) he cited Moses and the magicians of Egypt." After living in Maryland Lumbrozo found nothing unlawful in this honest expression of belief. As for what might have been a matter of law in the situation, he hastened to add that he "said not anything scoffingly, or in derogation of Him Christians acknowledge for their Messias."[10] As a lawyer he seemed to know the law and his point was made. It was consistent with the tradition the ordinance embodied.

THE CARROLLS WITH LIBERTY

The evident hardiness of this enduring Maryland tradition attracted an historically destined family to Maryland. Charles Carroll could have looked on his mural coat of arms at his country estate in Ireland in 1687 and found great meaning in it. He was restless under the restraints which the English government was putting on him, largely because he was a Catholic; and the family legend, "Wherever with liberty," must have prompted him to flight, which was also suggested by the emblem of a hawk uprising. He was familiar with the story of Maryland and he must have felt that the tradition of religious freedom sown there nearly sixty years before still promised to bear fruit.[11] Had it not endured the vicissitudes of Puritan inroads? Liberty continued to recede in the British Isles, so he must go where he could find it. The following year he came to Maryland, bearing the office of attorney general, defender of the legal structure reared on the ordinance.

A year had hardly passed when the rewards of his decision drifted from reach. The Stuarts who had been restored to power in 1660 lost their popularity, largely because the successor of James II seemed determined to be a Catholic, something Parliament would never endure in its monarch. Parliament chose in that year 1688 not another Puritan Revolution, but a Glorious Revolution, which put the Protestants William and Mary of the Netherlands on the throne of England. All came about with little or no bloodshed, but for Charles Carroll it was to be a brutal defeat. The Bill of Rights which Parliament passed became a political death warrant for a man as intent on the process of law as the members of the first Maryland Assembly had been. Something of the spirit of religious freedom, however, lingered on in spite of the rising supremacy of the crown over the Maryland colony. Carroll was deprived of his office and of a vote in the assembly, but he could speak up in court against the innovations which were harassing his fellow Catholics. The lingering liberality of Maryland did not begrudge him the opportunity of enlarging his investments and enhancing his family fortunes, which he proceeded to do. His success enabled him to send his son Charles to St. Omer's College which he had himself attended. Maryland law enforcement tolerantly looked the other way when the younger Carroll and other Catholic students departed from America contrary to a law against Catholic education.

While Charles was in Europe finishing his philosophical studies his father died. The younger Carroll had hoped to advance to the study of law in London, but he was needed immediately at home. He was also pessimistic about the future of a Catholic lawyer in eighteenth-century Maryland. This disappointment hung over the whole of his remaining lifetime. The unfavorable events and persecutions of the times left their scars on his sensitiveness as a Catholic. Other Maryland Catholics still held out hope. They petitioned the assembly in 1740 to restore the rights that the ordinance had guaranteed, but to no avail. Maryland was not in fact the vigorous, independent palatinate the early Calverts had strengthened. All were sadly reminded of this tragedy when Charles Calvert apostatized to the Church of England. Bitter though he was, Charles Carroll must have still hoped for a better day. He sent his son, also named Charles, one day to be known as Charles Carroll of Carrollton, to St. Omer's for his training, and he encouraged him to study law. In this third Charles the younger, sheltered from the harsh realities of dissent which oppressed his father, hope grew strong in his own future in Maryland.

In his desperation the elder Carroll began to talk of moving from Maryland to the more favorable environment of the French American colonies of the west. Charles wrote his father from Europe that this would be unwise and contrary to his own deep attachment to Maryland. As for his complaints against the government's discrimination, he reminded his father of the early Maryland laws and the liberties they guaranteed. It was only when he returned to America, however, that he saw that there was no proprietor worthy to defend them nor enough influence among the Catholic minority to get a hearing. Yet, as time went on, he became aware that other sects also resented the effect of established Anglicanism on their beliefs and especially on their taxes. On a merely political basis many Americans were becoming uneasy at the way the autonomy of the colony had slipped away. They began to speak of action when they saw the unfavorable shift of George III's tax and trade policy for the American colonies.

Long before, the farsighted Charles Carroll of Carrollton agreed that what had taken place in 1638 should come about on a grander scale for the freedom, not only of Maryland, but of all the colonies. Only then would there be a resurrection of the spirit of the ordinance.

So political and religious freedom came about with means too complex for the contemporary observer or the twentieth-century historian conclusively to explain. In the drama of revolution that unfolded, Maryland played her part, and the Carrolls were her most convincing protagonists. Charles Carroll's cousin helped formulate the Maryland bill for religious freedom, he himself signed the Declaration of Independence, and another cousin, Daniel, helped draft the First Amendment and signed the Constitution. Another cousin, John Carroll, first Catholic bishop of the United States, experienced in his career the benefit that came to the church when written law made the state delicate and reserved in its dealing with the church. The hawk upraised on the Carroll coat of arms could rest; Maryland had brought back its ancient freedom. Its inhabitants would have all their rights and liberties.

CONCLUSION

RELIGIOUS toleration in Maryland is usually represented by historians on a much narrower basis than has been undertaken in the foregoing pages. These writings give attention to the written prescriptions in the Toleration Act of 1649 and describe practices and incidents touching on religious liberty. On the whole, the greatest consideration is given to the Calverts, who are carefully measured against our American ideal of religious toleration. The picture thus presented stands firmly on the selected documents, but implications are suggested which are not satisfactorily formulated or substantiated. This limitation seems in some measure to be due to the narrow basis on which study of Maryland has proceeded.

By concentrating analysis at vital points in the broader development of religious and political freedom in Maryland, more certain implications and conclusions have emerged. Of great importance is the fact that Maryland Catholics in the first Maryland assemblies were drawing on a hard-won tradition, which was neither Spanish, nor European, but distinctively an English Catholic creation. This tradition possessed in clearer form the fundamental principles which characterized it. The church and state were viewed, not so much in terms of union or separation, but as two sovereignties. The essential functions of each were clearly recognized, and any usurpation by either was detected by this essential reference. In a distinctive manner, this tradition demanded reserve in the exercise of authority by each sovereignty in mixed temporal and spiritual matters. The religious and political freedom of the citizen became the overriding consideration in reaching a practical settlement. Because the Catholic's religious liberty had in the past suffered from the absolute monarchical political form, he came to hold fast to the democratic theory on the origin and exercise of civil authority as Bellarmine and others explained it.

The Englishman had an ancient sense of personal liberty, which in the tradition of the Magna Charta included both religious and civil freedom. Because the English Catholic since More's day was severely afflicted in his sense of personal liberty, he became most sensitive at this point. Any exercise of authority by either church or state had to deal gently in this area. From the positive standpoint of the Maryland assemblymen, this sensitive point of consciousness prompted them to insist on the limitation of political authority by democratic restraints. The same awareness made the assemblymen reserved in any matter which might in any way coerce conscience or tamper with one's "faith with God."

We have seen that this delicate complex of principles in the English Catholic tradition was the outgrowth of a unique historical experience. The tradition could not be written off in any legalistic formula. Yet in Maryland its principles accurately responded to situations which involved religious and political freedom. Church and state were honored as true sovereignties. The citizen, by the power of the assembly, proudly realized that the state had its origin in him, whose liberty it should preserve. The state had a reverent regard for his freedom to pursue his spiritual destiny in God.

Out of this background came the beginnings of religious toleration in Maryland. The experience by a large number of Englishmen as well as the leadership and thought of a few brought it into existence in the mother country as well as in America. The great launching period in the New World occurred when the Maryland Assembly passed the ordinance of 1639. The events of a hundred years before and after the ordinance naturally emerge as prologue and epilogue to this momentous event. After a detailed analysis and accounting of those days of the ordinance, we should be able to see why it holds a central position in the development of toleration in Maryland.

This prominence of the Maryland Ordinance of 1639 logically demands a reconsideration of the role of the proprietors and the Toleration Act of 1649. Calvert did not at all times speak for the Maryland Catholics. Indeed, by and large he was not representative of their mind on a large range of matters. Neither is the Puritan-tinged Toleration Act of 1649 representative of the Catholics, who had lost their dominant position in the assembly by that time.

One other adjustment must also be made. Greater exactness must be attached to the general term *toleration* in Maryland by reference to the ordinance of 1639. Whatever subsequent practices or laws had kinship with this legislation should be seen in the light of the tradition which created the ordinance. There is evidence that this tradition persisted, at least among Catholics in Maryland, up to the days of the Constitutional Convention. All of this suggests that we may have today a distinctive tradition among Catholics, the outcome of their American experience which began in the precedents of the 1639 ordinance.

The Catholic tradition in Maryland, however, encountered others of a different origin, the Puritan, the Anglican, the Quaker, and the various evangelical Protestant traditions. Toleration as understood by these sects was greatly affected by their notions of church and state as well as their philosophical understandings of political institutions. By the investigation of these areas, the pluralistic society of seventeenth-century Maryland can be more surely understood in what was the foremost concern of the early Americans, religious and political freedom. The present study suggests that some agreement among the sects may have developed during the colonial period in Maryland, bringing about adjustments with the starting points which the ordinance of 1639 had established.

The pattern of beginnings in political and religious freedom in Maryland was unique. Within this period and its background, no single generation was without its own particular burden to be borne in the advance of man's freedom. European nations had sought in vain to fix once and for all a church-state "system" with accompanying practices which would be valid for subsequent generations. Thanks to the vigor of minorities and to the very nature of man's political reality, such systems did not stand as irreproachable conquerors. What prevailed eventually were insights into valid principles of freedom, which won devoted adherents. These disciples of liberty left to subsequent generations a tradition of such principles. This seemed a humbler but more lasting contribution than a "system" which promised some easy and inflexible solution to the problem of freedom in society. The story we have considered tells us that men must not only labor to find truth in the application of their principles, but they must be prepared to suffer for what they inherit.

NOTES

INTRODUCTION

[1] *Calvert Papers* (Baltimore, 1889), 35.

[2] "The Proprietary Province as a Form of Colonial Government,"*American Historical Review,* II (July, 1897), p. 654.

I: GOD'S SERVANT FIRST

[1] Among others, see Charles M. Andrews, *Our Earliest Colonial Settlements* (New York, 1933), pp. 165–166.

[2] *Archives of Maryland,* Ed. by William H. Browne, *et al.* (Baltimore, 1883—), I, pp. 82–83. Hereafter cited as *Archives.*

[3] In the general histories of Maryland and studies of the development of toleration, mention is made of the events concerned with the Ordinance of 1639. These works provide an excellent basis for carrying the study of toleration farther ahead by an effort at understanding the meaning of church and state.

[4] Matthew Page Andrews, *The Founding of Maryland* (New York, 1933), p. 156; Bradley T. Johnson, *The Foundation of Maryland and the Origin of the Act Concerning Religion of April 21, 1649* (Baltimore, 1883), p. 8.

[5] David Mathew, *Catholicism in England, 1535–1935* (London, 1936), pp. 7, 24, 32.

[6] Raymond W. Chambers, *Sir Thomas More* (Westminster, Md., 1949), p. 23. See also the author's Prologue and Epilogue. Within twenty years of his death, More's works had gone through many editions.

[7] A. I. Lindsay, review of J. W. Allen's *A History of Political Thought in the Sixteenth Century* (London, 1951), in *American Political Science Review,* 23 (August, 1929), 156.

[8] J. W. Allen, *op. cit.,* Part 2, chs. 1, 2, 7.

[9] *Archives,* I, 82–83.

[10] *The Prince,* trans. N. H. Thomson, *Harvard Classics* (New York, 1910), vol. 36, pp. 57, 23 ff.

[11] William Roper, *The Lyfe of Sir Thomas Moore,* ed. E. V. Hitchcock (London, 1935), pp. 7–8.

[12] *Ibid.,* p. 118. Chambers supports this interpretation by More's correspondence with Cromwell, cf. *op. cit.,* p. 194.

[13] Chambers, *op. cit.,* p. 194.

[14] *Ibid.*

[15] *Ibid.*, p. 337.

[16] *Ibid.*, p. 340.

[17] In saying this I do not wish to oversimplify the inherent difficulty of *Utopia's* literary genre. We can never conclude that More believed in all the practices of the Utopians as a basis of social reform; but in describing these practices More is indulging in social criticism, and by further analysis and illation we can often discover the principles which underlie his criticism. In addition to *Utopia*, we can look to other writings of More and to the record of his own life for further enlightenment. See Edward L. Surtz's excellent discussion of these problems in *The Praise of Pleasure* (Cambridge, 1957), chapters 1 and 16. A significant observation and point of view of the author is that More's work, in contrast to *Praise of Folly* by Erasmus, is constructive.

[18] J. Messner, *Social Ethics: Natural Law in the Modern World* (St. Louis, 1949), p. 83. See Reinhold Niebuhr's discussion of Luther's "defeatism in the realm of social politics, and of his uncritical attitude toward the power of government," in *The Nature and Destiny of Man* (New York, 1946), pp. 195, 278; and chapter 7 for a general discussion of the Reformation.

[19] *The "Utopia" of Sir Thomas More, in Latin from the Edition of March 1518, and in English from the First Edition of Ralph Robynson's Translation in 1551* (Oxford, 1895), pp. 184–186. Subsequent references to *Utopia* are to this edition and its Latin text. My own rendering in English is in reference to this rather than any of the published translations.

[20] In Surtz, *op. cit.*, p. 110.

[21] *Utopia*, pp. 135–136.

[22] *St. Thomas Aquinas on Kingship*, trans. by Gerald B. Phelan (Toronto, 1949), pp. 11–13, 55–58; Allen, *op. cit.*, part 2, chapter 1; Heinrich A. Rommen, *The State in Catholic Thought* (St. Louis, 1945), pp. 539–540.

[23] See Edward L. Surtz, S.J., *The Praise of Wisdom* (Chicago, 1957), chapter 2, "God: Reason and Faith."

[24] *Utopia*, pp. 270, 272–273.

[25] *Ibid.*, p. 271; *The Apologye of Syr Thomas More, Knyght*, edited by Arthur I. Taft (London: Early English Text Society, 1930), pp. lxvi ff., and 131 ff.; William Roper, *The Lyfe of Sir Thomas Moore*, p. 35. Father Surtz seems substantially to agree with the interpretation followed here: "In a word, More foresaw a state of affairs in which all Christian sects would live in a state of mutual tolerance and would be free to maintain their churches and to preach their doctrines in peace," *The Praise of Wisdom*, p. 75.

[26] This is revealed principally in the consistency with which More always stresses the problem of public peace and in his recollection of the Knights' War and Peasants' War.

[27] *Apologye*, pp. lxvi–lxvii; cf. particularly Taft's remarks.

[28] *Ibid.*, pp. lxxvi ff.; Chambers, *op. cit.*, pp. 274 ff.

[29] Chambers uses the term conservative in interpreting More's thought. For another view, see Russell Ames, *Citizen Thomas More and His Utopia* (Princeton, N. J., 1949), pp. 18 ff.

[30] *Church and State Through the Centuries*, trans. and ed. by Sidney Z. Ehler

and John B. Morrall (Westminster, Md., 1954); pp. 11–12 have short passages from Gelasius and others relevant to this discussion.

³¹ *Ibid.*

³² *Tractatus iv,* 11, in *Epistolae Romanorum Pontificum Genuinae,* ed. by Andreas Thiel (Brunsbergae, 1868), I, 567–568.

³³ Rommen, *op. cit.,* pp. 539–40.

³⁴ Pierre Janelle, *The Catholic Reformation* (Milwaukee, 1949), p. 108.

³⁵ "Charles VI's Address at Brussells, 1555," *Readings in European History,* ed. by James H. Robinson (Boston, 1906), vol. II, 167.

II: THE KING'S GOOD SERVANTS

¹ *A Popular History of the Reformation* (Garden City, N. Y., 1956), p. 299.

² J. H. Pollen in the *Catholic Encyclopedia* (New York, 1907), XI, 730–731.

³ *A treatise concerning the Broken Succession of the Crown of England* (London, 1655), p. 20.

⁴ *Certain Reasons,* p. 55; W. K. Jordan, *The Development of Toleration in England* (Cambridge, Mass., 1932), I, 390–391.

⁵ *The Sixteenth Century,* p. 205.

⁶ Luigi Sturzo, *Church and State* (New York, 1939), p. 224. For *Regnans in Excelsis* see Philip Hughes, *The Reformation in England* (London, 1950–1954), III, 418–420. Italics added.

⁷ *Allen's Defense of English Catholics* (St. Louis, 1914), I, 81, 72, 73.

⁸ Cited in J. W. Allen, *The Sixteenth Century,* p. 207.

⁹ *Op. cit.,* II, 12–13.

¹⁰ *Select Statutes and Other Constitutional Documents,* ed. by G. W. Prothero (Oxford, 1934), p. 259.

¹¹ *The Political Works of James I,* ed. by Charles H. McIlwain (Cambridge, Mass., 1918), p. liii.

¹² Prothero, *op. cit.,* p. 259.

¹³ McIlwain, *op. cit.,* p. liii.

¹⁴ For Bellarmine's words see Xavier-M. LeBachelet (ed.), *Auctarium Bellarminianum* (Paris, 1913), p. 235; James Brodrick, *The Life and Times of Blessed Robert Cardinal Bellarmine, 1542–1621* (London, 1928), II, p. 166. See also Sturzo, *op. cit.,* p. 250. On the problem of Bellarmine as treated here, see John Courtney Murray, S.J., "St. Robert Bellarmine on the Indirect Power," in *Theological Studies,* IX (December, 1948).

¹⁵ Thomas Hughes, *The History of the Society of Jesus in North America: Text* (New York, 1917), I, p. 205.

III: WHAT MARYLAND WAS WITHIN

¹ Charles M. Andrews, *The Colonial Period of American History* (New Haven, Conn., 1937), II, pp. 277–278.

2 William H. Browne, *George and Cecilius Calvert* (New York, 1890), gives an account of the known details of the Lords Baltimore.

3 Prothero, *Select Statutes*, pp. 313–314.

4 Cf. *Dictionary of English Catholics*, ed. by Joseph Gillow (London, 1895–1912), I, pp. 71–72.

5 C. M. Andrews, *Colonial Period*, I, pp. 79–80.

6 *Archives*, III, p. 17.

7 *Ibid.*, pp. 4 ff. give the Charter text.

8 *Colonial Period*, II, pp. 277–278.

9 Osgood, *loc. cit.*, p. 645.

10 *Archives*, III, p. 12.

11 William King, "Lord Baltimore and His Freedom in Granting Religious Toleration," *American Catholic Historical Society Records*, XXXII (Dec., 1921), p. 298.

12 *Church and State in Maryland* (Baltimore, 1892), p. 11.

13 *Archives*, III, p. 12.

14 *Ibid.*, p. 6.

15 *Ibid.*, p. 19.

16 T. Hughes, *The History of the Society of Jesus in North America: Documents* (New York, 1917), I, no. 4.

17 Clayton C. Hall, *Narratives of Early Maryland* (New York, 1910), pp. 16–22.

18 J. Moss Ives, *The Ark and the Dove* (New York, 1936), p. 146. For a similar directive, see *Archives*, III, p. 210.

19 Hall, *Narratives*, pp. 5–10.

IV: ACCORDING TO THE GREAT CHARTER

1 Hall, *Narratives*, pp. 5–6.

2 *Archives*, IV, pp. 35–36.

3 *Ibid.*

4 *Ibid.*, pp. 36–37.

5 *Ibid.*, I, p. 17.

6 St. George L. Sioussat, *The English Statutes in Maryland* (Baltimore, 1903), p. 475.

7 *Studies in the History of American Law* (New York, 1930), p. 475.

8 This led to permanent exclusion of the clergy from the assembly later on.

9 *Archives*, I, pp. 136, 148, 175–176.

10 *Ibid.*, III, pp. 50 ff.

11 *Ibid.*, I, p. 8.

12 *Ibid.*, I, p. 9.

13 *Ibid.*

V: THEIR RIGHTS AND LIBERTIES

1 *Calvert Papers*, pp. 189–190.

2 *Ibid.*, p. 173.

3 *Archives*, I, pp. 174–175.

4 *Ibid.*, pp. 41, 73, 75.

5 *Ibid.*, p. 83.

6 *Ibid.*, p. 81.

7 *Ibid.*, p. 82.

8 *Calvert Papers*, p. 173.

9 *Archives*, I, p. 84.

10 *Calvert Papers*, p. 172.

11 *Ibid.*, p. 171.

12 *Ibid.*, pp. 157–169 contain Copley's letter.

13 William T. Russell, *Maryland Land and Sanctuary* (Baltimore, 1907), has a discussion of the various charters and their references to church rights.

14 Placing a distinct act for church liberties in the ordinance confirms this interpretation.

15 *Archives*, I, pp. 71–72.

16 *Ibid.*, p. 84.

17 *Ibid.*, p. 75.

18 *Ibid.*, p. 77.

VI: THOSE PROFESSING BELIEF

1 *Calvert Papers*, pp. 158–159.

2 *Bullarum Diplomatum et Privilegiorum Sanctorum Romanorum Pontificum* (Taurinensis, 1868), XIII, 530–537.

3 *Calvert Papers*, p. 166.

4 *Records of the English Province of the Society of Jesus*, ed. by Henry Foley (London, 1875–1883), II, 420.

5 *Ibid.*, 423.

6 *Archives*, I, pp. 244 ff. contains the Toleration Act.

7 *Ibid.*, pp. 277–278.

8 *Archives*, XLI, pp. 132–133, 144–146, 171, 263, 566–567; these passages give the essential story of Father Fitzherbert.

9 *Ibid.*, pp. 104, 286, 322.

10 Cf. M. P. Andrews' discussion in *Founding of Maryland*, pp. 95–96, 136–137.

11 Ellen Hart Smith's *Charles Carroll of Carrollton* (Cambridge, Mass., 1942) is the most satisfactory biography of Carroll and has been most useful in this passage.

BIBLIOGRAPHY

PRIMARY SOURCES

ALLEN, William. *Allen's Defense of English Catholics.* St. Louis, 1914.

———. *A True, Sincere and Modest Defense of English Catholiques.* Ingolstadt, 1584.

Archives of Maryland. 67 vols. Edited by William Hand Browne, *et al.* Baltimore, 1883.

BELLARMINE, Robert. *Auctarium Bellarminianum.* Edited by Xavier-M. LaBachelet. Paris, 1913.

Bullarum Diplomatum et Privilegiorum Sanctorum Romanorum Pontificum. 24 vols. Edited by Augustae Taurinorum, *et al.* Rome, 1857–1872.

Calvert Papers. Maryland Historical Society Fund Publication No. 18. Baltimore, 1889.

CARROLL, Charles. *Unpublished Letters of.* Edited by Thomas M. Field. New York, 1902.

Church and State Through the Centuries. Edited by Sidney Z. Ehler and John B. Morrall. Westminster, Md., 1954.

Epistolae Romanorum Pontificum Genuinae. Edited by Andreas Thiel. Brunsbergae, 1868.

The History of the Society of Jesus in North America: Documents. 2 vols. Edited by Thomas Hughes. New York, 1917.

JAMES I. *The Political Works of James I.* Edited by Charles H. McIlwain. Cambridge, 1918.

MACHIAVELLI, Nicholo. *The Prince.* Translated by N. H. Thomson; The Harvard Classics. Vol. 36. New York, 1910.

MORE, Thomas. *The Apologye of Syr Thomas More, Knyght*. Edited by Arthur I. Taft. Oxford, 1930.

———. *The "Utopia" of Sir Thomas More, in Latin from the Edition of March 1518, and in English from the First Edition of Ralph Robynson's Translation in 1551*. Edited by J. H. Lupton. Oxford, 1895.

Narratives of Early Maryland. Edited by Clayton C. Hall. New York, 1910.

PERSONS, Robert. *De Persecutione Anglicana*. Romae, 1582.

———. *Elizabethae, Angliae Reginae*. 1592.

———. *A Treatise Concerning the Broken Succession of the Crown of England*. London, 1655.

———. *A Treatise of Three Conversions of England from Paganisme to Christian Religion*. 2 vols. 1603–1604.

Records of the English Province of the Society of Jesus. 7 vols. Edited by Henry Foley, S. J. London, 1875–1883.

ROPER, William. *The Life of Sir Thomas More*. Edited by E. V. Hitchcock. London, 1935.

ST. THOMAS AQUINAS. *On Kingship*. Translated by Gerald B. Phelan. Toronto, 1949.

Select Statutes and Other Constitutional Documents Illustrative of the Reign of Elizabeth and James I. Edited by G. W. Prothero. Oxford, 1934.

SECONDARY SOURCES

ALLEN, John W. *A History of Political Thought in the Sixteenth Century*. London, 1951.

AMES, Russell A. *Citizen Thomas More and his Utopia*. Princeton, 1949.

ANDREWS, Charles M. *The Colonial Period of American History*. 4 vols. New Haven, 1937.

————. *Our Earliest Colonial Settlements: Their Diversity of Origin and Later Characteristics.* New York, 1933.

ANDREWS, Matthew Page. *The Founding of Maryland.* New York, 1933.

————. *History of Maryland: Province and State.* New York, 1929.

————. "Separation of Church and State in Maryland," *Catholic Historical Review,* XXI (July, 1935), 164–176.

BOZMAN, John Leeds. *The History of Maryland.* 2 vols. Baltimore, 1837.

BRODRICK, James. *The Life and Work of Blessed Robert Francis Cardinal Bellarmine 1542–1621.* 2 vols. London, 1928.

CARLYLE, Alexander J., and Robert W. *A History of Medieval Political Theory in the West.* 6 vols. London, 1903–1928.

The Catholic Encyclopedia. 15 vols. Edited by Charles G. Herbermann *et al.* New York, 1907.

CHAMBERS, Raymond W. *Sir Thomas More.* Westminster, Md., 1949.

CLARKE, Mary Patterson. *Parliamentary Privilege in the American Colonies.* New Haven, 1943.

COBB, Sanford H. *The Rise of Religious Liberty in America.* New York, 1902.

DENNIS, Alfred P. "Lord Baltimore's Struggle with the Jesuits, 1634–1649." *Proceedings of the American Historical Association.* Vol. I.

DUNNING, William A. *A History of Political Theories from Luther to Montesquieu.* New York, 1905.

GOODMAN, Abram Vossen. *American Overture: Jewish Rights In Colonial Times.* Philadelphia, 1947.

GRIFFITH, Thomas W. *Sketches of the Early History of Maryland.* Baltimore, 1821.

GUILDAY, Peter K. *The Life and Times of John Carroll.* New York, 1922.

HAILE, Martin. *An Elizabethan Cardinal, William Allen.* London, 1914.

HUGHES, Philip. *A Popular History of the Reformation.* New York, 1956.

———. *The Reformation In England.* 3 vols. London, 1950–1954.

———. *Rome and the Counter-Reformation in England.* London, 1942.

HUGHES, Thomas, S.J. *The History of the Society of Jesus in North America, Text.* 2 vols. New York, 1917.

IVES, J. Moss. *The Ark and the Dove.* New York, 1936.

JANELLE, Pierre. *The Catholic Reformation.* Milwaukee, 1949.

JOHNSON, Bradley T. *The Foundation of Maryland and the Origin of the Act Concerning Religion of April 21, 1649.* Baltimore, 1883.

JORDAN, W. K. *The Development of Toleration in England.* 3 vols. Cambridge, 1932.

KING, William. "Lord Baltimore and His Freedom in Granting Religious Toleration," *American Catholic Historical Society Records,* XXXII (Dec., 1921), 295–313.

A Literary and Biographical History, or Bibliographical Dictionary of the English Catholics, from the Breach with Rome, in 1534, to the Present Time. 5 vols. Edited by Joseph Gillow. London, 1885–1902.

McLAUGHLIN, Andrew Cunningham. *The Foundations of American Constitutionalism.* New York, 1933.

MATHEW, David. *Catholicism in England, 1535–1935.* London, 1936.

MELVILLE, Annabelle M. *John Carroll of Baltimore: Founder of the American Catholic Hierarchy.* New York, 1955.

MERENESS, Newton D. *Maryland as a Proprietary Province.* New York, 1901.

MESSNER, J. *Social Ethics: Natural Law in the Modern World.* St. Louis, 1949.

MILLER, Perry. *The New England Mind: The Seventeenth Century.* New York, 1939.

MORRIS, John G. *The Lords Baltimore.* Baltimore, 1874.

MORRIS, Richard B. *Studies in the History of American Law: With Special Reference to the Seventeenth and Eighteenth Centuries.* New York, 1930.

MURRAY, John Courtney, S. J. "St. Robert Bellarmine on the Indirect Power," *Theological Studies,* IX (Dec. 1948), 491–535.

NIEBUHR, Reinhold. *The Nature and Destiny of Man: A Christian Interpretation.* New York, 1946.

NUESSE, Celestine Joseph. *The Social Thought of American Catholics, 1634–1829.* Washington, D. C., 1945.

OSGOOD, Herbert L. "The Proprietary Province as a Form of Colonial Government," *American Historical Review,* II (July, 1897), 644–665.

PARKE, Francis Neal. "Witchcraft in Maryland," *Maryland Historical Magazine,* XXXI (Dec., 1936), 271–298.

PETRIE, George. *Church and State in Maryland.* Baltimore, 1892.

The Political Works of James I. Edited by Charles H. McIlwain. Cambridge, 1918.

ROMAGOSA, Edward J., S. J. "The Church-State Theory of Pope St. Gelasius I and Its Influence on Later Ages up to the End of the Twelfth Century." Unpublished MS. Louvain, College of St. Albert, 1955.

ROMMEN, Heinrich A. *The State in Catholic Thought: A Treatise in Political Philosophy.* St. Louis, 1945.

ROWLAND, Kate M. *The Life of Charles Carroll of Carrollton, 1737–1832: With his Correspondence and Public Papers.* New York, 1898.

RUSSELL, Elbert. *The History of Quakerism.* New York, 1943.

RUSSELL, William T. *Maryland Land and Sanctuary.* Baltimore, 1907.

Scharf, Thomas J. *History of Maryland*. 3 vols. Baltimore, 1879.

Semmes, Ralph. *Crime and Punishment in Early Maryland*. Baltimore, 1938.

Shea, John G. *A History of the Catholic Church*. 4 vols. New York, 1886.

Simon, Yves R. *Philosophy of Democratic Government*. Chicago, 1951.

Sioussat, St. George L. *The English Statutes in Maryland*. Baltimore, 1903.

Smith, Ellen Hart. *Charles Carroll of Carrollton*. Cambridge, 1942.

Steiner, B. C. *Beginnings of Maryland, 1631–1639*. Baltimore, 1903.

————. "The First Lord Baltimore and His Colonial Project." *American Historical Association, Annual Reports, 1905*. Vol. I.

Stockbridge, Henry. *Archives of Maryland as Illustrating the Spirit of the Times of the Early Colonists*. Baltimore, 1886.

Stokes, Anson P. *Church and State in the United States*. 3 vols. New York, 1950.

Stratemeir, George B. *Thomas Cornwaleys Commissioner and Counsellor of Maryland*. Washington, D. C., 1922.

Sturzo, Luigi. *Church and State*. New York, 1939.

Surtz, Edward L., S. J. "Logic in Utopia," *Philological Quarterly*, XXIX (Oct., 1950), 389–401.

————. *The Praise of Pleasure: Philosophy, Education and Communism in More's Utopia*. Cambridge, 1957.

————. *The Praise of Wisdom: A Commentary on the Religious and Moral Problems and Backgrounds of St. Thomas More's Utopia*. Chicago, 1957.

————. "Thomas More and the Great Books," *Philological Quarterly* XXXII (Jan., 1953), 43–51.

STREETER, Sebastian F. *Papers Relating to the Early History of Maryland*. Baltimore, 1876.

WERLINE, Albert W. *Problems of Church and State in Maryland During the Seventeenth and Eighteenth Centuries*. South Lancaster, Mass., 1948.

WROTH, L. C. "The First Sixty Years of the Church of England in Maryland, 1632–1692," *Maryland Historical Magazine*, XI (March, 1916), 1–41.

INDEX